The Dispossessed

To Héloïse, Adèle and Nine

The Dispossessed
The Working Classes and their Instinct for Survival

Christophe Guilluy

Translated by Andrew Brown

polity

Originally published in French as *Les dépossédés. L'instinct de survie des classes populaires* © Flammarion, 2022, 2023

This English translation © Polity Press, 2025

Polity Press
65 Bridge Street
Cambridge CB2 1UR, UK

Polity Press
111 River Street
Hoboken, NJ 07030, USA

All rights reserved. Except for the quotation of short passages for the purpose of criticism and review, no part of this publication may be reproduced, stored in a retrieval system or transmitted, in any form or by any means, electronic, mechanical, photocopying, recording or otherwise, without the prior permission of the publisher.

ISBN-13: 978-1-5095-6845-1 – hardback
ISBN-13: 978-1-5095-6846-8 – paperback

A catalogue record for this book is available from the British Library.

Library of Congress Control Number: 2024950506

Typeset in 11 on 14pt Warnock Pro
by Cheshire Typesetting Ltd, Cuddington, Cheshire
Printed and bound in Great Britain by CPI Group (UK) Ltd, Croydon

The publisher has used its best endeavours to ensure that the URLs for external websites referred to in this book are correct and active at the time of going to press. However, the publisher has no responsibility for the websites and can make no guarantee that a site will remain live or that the content is or will remain appropriate.

Every effort has been made to trace all copyright holders, but if any have been overlooked the publisher will be pleased to include any necessary credits in any subsequent reprint or edition.

For further information on Polity, visit our website: politybooks.com

Contents

Introduction 1

Part I The sea 3

1 Access to the sea 5
   Back to square one 8
   The 'unbowed' bourgeoisie and the sense of heritage 16

2 The forbidden city 18
   Urban cloning 21
   The cemetery of the political left 22
   The forbidden city 25

3 The social imprint 30
   Ecologically responsible, socially irresponsible 32
   The peril of social distancing 37

Part II The fog 41

4 Cinema 45
   From narrative to cinema 46

Their cinema	48
The transclass, an Oscar-worthy role	52
The realm of whiners	58
5 'There is no majority'	64
The language that renders people invisible	64
The parent company is Netflix	67
The utopia of a new people	72
Coming out of one's reserve	74
6 Apocalypse now	77
Act I Enter the Prince of Darkness	77
Act II The announcement of dark times	83
Part III The horizon	**87**
7 The radical nature of ordinary life	91
The survival instinct	93
The electoral hard discount and abstention	95
8 Not against but elsewhere	99
A dialogue of the deaf	101
And what about a summit conference on living conditions?	105
9 Return to the centre	108
The idiot	109
The West doesn't need anyone else's help to decline	111
It's now okay to be pragmatic	115
Epilogue	118
Notes	120

Introduction

It makes a strange impression, overall: the dominant classes have never monopolized as much power, accumulated as much wealth, and controlled the political-media narrative as much as they do now; and yet, at the same time, they have never seemed so feeble, incompetent, and ridiculous. For their part, the working classes, although economically and culturally diminished, have never been a source of so much anxiety.

At the end of the twentieth century there was a 'phoney war' that produced a protest unlike any of the social movements of previous centuries. It was not led by any party, union, or leader, but by ordinary people. Its deep roots – and this is what made it so special – were not material so much as existential.

This protest was not driven by class consciousness, but by the sense that people have been dispossessed of their prerogatives, and gradually shunted out to the edge of the world. Its strength and serenity are due to its long-term nature. It disturbs the proponents both of a perpetual present and of permanent agitation. Its immaterial dimension makes it unstoppable, and above all it evades the grasp of the ruling elites, who had got used to settling everything with a wave of the cheque book.

This movement is not a remake of *Les Misérables:* it is much more than that. It is the movement of the dispossessed – of a mass of common people that gained a will of its own and was no longer content to comply with the directives of those who tell it how to live – or just how to survive – and how to behave.

Over time, this irresistible and protean protest has spread to the majority of people. Driven by the desire to impose a return to the social and cultural realities of ordinary life, it shatters the story told by those who had promised us the best of all possible worlds.

Part I
The sea

1
Access to the sea

It was on the night of 7–8 June 1936 that the Confédération Générale du Travail and the employers of the Confédération Générale de la production française[1] signed an historic agreement with the government, the so-called Matignon Agreements, setting the working week at forty hours, raising wages, establishing trade union rights and giving employees paid leave. A month earlier, the electoral success of a coalition of left-wing parties, united under the banner of the 'Popular Front', had raised hopes for an improvement in working and living conditions. This aspiration triggered an unprecedented movement of strikes and factory occupations throughout France. One thousand two hundred picket lines sprang up, and it is estimated that two million workers walked out. Four days after this agreement, the General Secretary of the French Communist Party, Maurice Thorez, declared that 'you have to be able to end a strike when you've got what you wanted'. On 20 June 1936, the Popular Front government announced that it would grant two weeks' paid vacation to all employees.

Workers would be able to 'get to the seaside' for a break. But the vast majority of workers obviously did not have the money to afford a vacation, or even to travel. At that time, a car was an almost unaffordable luxury – a means of transport primarily reserved for the upper and lower middle classes. Aware of this reality, the Undersecretary of State for the Organization of Leisure and Sports, Léo Lagrange, imposed reduced-price tickets on reluctant railway companies. Put on sale on 3 August 1936, the 'workers' tickets for paid vacations' allowed people to travel by train at a sixty per cent discount, provided they travelled at least 200 kilometres – a distance that was not chosen at random, since it opened the beaches of the English Channel to the working-class strongholds of the Paris region and the north of France. People immediately flocked to the railway stations. The atmosphere was joyful; the jubilation, the cheerfulness, the broad smiles would be abundantly immortalized by film-makers and photographers (Robert Doisneau and Henri Cartier-Bresson in particular). Access to the seaside, once the reserve of the privileged, marked a cultural shift.

Let us be clear, however, that these now iconic scenes are misleading. Contrary to such rose-tinted images, the Popular Front's measures did not trigger a rush to the seaside. In reality, it is estimated that, of the ten million French people now able to take two weeks' paid leave, barely five per cent were able to take a vacation.[2] The new holidaymakers did not have the means to go very far, and most of them chose destinations very close to home. For example, those from the Île-de-France region around Paris went to the riverbanks of the Seine or the Marne. However, those who did decide to go beyond the 200 kilometres laid down by the so-called 'Léo Lagrange tickets' opted for the seaside. Workers went to the beaches of the English Channel, the Mediterranean and the Atlantic. Many of them had never seen the sea, so they logically headed for the fashionable resorts they had heard about, especially those with train stations. In a few days, middle-class holiday resorts – Cabourg, Deauville, Houlgate, Le Touquet, Dinard, and La Baule in the north, and Nice, Cannes, Arcachon, and Biarritz in the south – witnessed a population explosion.

The seaside, the swimming, the deep clear waters, the silvery reflections: they were all there. But so was social otherness. The eruption of the working classes into these places of bourgeois endogamy caused unprecedented tensions.

The massive arrival of the working classes in these small seaside resorts triggered a culture shock. For the first time, the rich would have to share their playgrounds. Picnics, *pétanque*, camping: the working-class lifestyle emerged in places that had always been governed by the norms and customs of the privileged. This enforced cohabitation triggered criticism of those who were contemptuously called 'paid holidaymakers', and whose bathing suits and vest tops were mocked.

The bourgeoisie was soon thinking about what to do next; a few years later they had reorganized their vacation spots. After the war, the seasonal provision of holiday places was segmented. Luxury villas for the middle classes, low-end rentals for low-income earners. In addition, the former were helped by elected officials, who authorized (or not) the installation of campsites in their municipalities. For their part, from the 1960s, the ultra-rich opted for a radical separation: they now holidayed on board yachts, the market for which exploded during the *Trente Glorieuses*,[3] as a riposte to the advent of mass tourism.

If paid vacations were one of the great social achievements of the working classes, access to the sea took on a highly symbolic dimension and went far beyond the social question. Access to the coasts, and to other distant landscapes, changed the horizon of the most modest classes, which had hitherto been limited to the places where they lived: the neighbourhoods and municipalities of the big industrial conurbations for workers, the countryside for those who dwelt in areas not as yet called 'rural'. Thus, access to the sea was more than a social advance; it also represented a cultural advance. In the summer of 1936, the working classes reached the horizon, broadened their field of vision, and made themselves visible, not only as the essential cogs of the economy, but also as an unavoidable cultural group.

Back to square one

More than eighty years later, in 2022, the small village of Caurel in Côtes-d'Armor was the scene of an attack. A holiday home was set on fire. The house was completely burned, except for the walls. There were two stencilled inscriptions, making a political statement: 'FLB' – a reference to the Front de libération de la Bretagne (Front for the Liberation of Brittany)[4] and the hundreds of attacks it had committed between 1966 and 2000. The local press was up in arms too: *Le Télégramme* asked: 'Should we fear a return of armed struggle in Brittany?'[5]

The newspaper noted that the threats had become increasingly overt over the last few months, in the form of damage and destruction, and an ultimatum signed 'FLB'. In January, another home in the same village, where sixty per cent of residences were holiday homes, was damaged – with the same graffiti.[6]

A few decades before, this type of action had been carried out in Corsica, when the FLNC[7] dynamited villas belonging to mainlanders or foreigners. Though fewer in number these days, the attacks have not disappeared from the island. On 7 April 2022, in Ghisonaccia, a mainlander's secondary residence was targeted. A gas bottle connected to an explosive device was found on site. The day before, another secondary residence, also belonging to mainlanders, had been partially destroyed in Canale-di-Verde. In addition, the inscriptions 'IFF' ('I Francesi Fora', 'French Go Home') sprang up all over the place.

In Corsica, where one in three homes is a secondary residence (a national record),[8] the proliferation of such residences is a very sensitive subject for locals, and one taken up in particular by nationalists. Mainland owners who stay for the holidays or rent out their property during the summer season, to the detriment of hoteliers, are in fact causing property prices to soar, often preventing young Corsican families from accessing housing.

This picture is the same across all the French coastlines. It raises a fundamental question, that of access to housing for young people and workers in these *zones tendues* (tense zones),[9] and ultimately the matter of the right to work, live and therefore find accommodation 'in one's own part of the country'.

Violent actions are only the tip of the iceberg of a protest that is tending to become more widespread. All over the coastline, from Brittany to the Basque coast, there are increasing numbers of demonstrations. Groups and elected officials are mobilizing to find legal means to curb the proliferation of secondary residences and the 'Airbnb tsunami' that comes with it.[10] While the walls in the Basque Country remind us that 'Euskal Herria Ez da Salgai' ('The Basque Country is not for sale'), it does not look as if the market mechanism is going to grind to a halt anytime soon: and that is because this shortage of housing supply is the direct consequence of a change in lifestyles, particularly those of the upper classes and wealthy retirees.

In Brittany as elsewhere, it is the bourgeoisie that is snapping up local real estate,[11] and the impact of this land grab is already being felt locally. La Couarde-sur-Mer, a village on the Île-de-Ré on France's Atlantic seaboard, with 1,200 inhabitants, lost half of its workforce over the last twenty years or so, and is struggling to prevent the closure of its school. Patrick Rayton, the mayor, sounds the alarm: 'The phenomenon is similar everywhere on the island. We currently have more than a hundred families waiting for a year-round rental!'[12] In Brittany, to limit the number of secondary residences, the 'Housing for All' team points out that, in this region, 'there are 330,000 empty homes for nine months out of twelve' and therefore proposes to place all of Brittany in a 'tense zone' in order to surcharge secondary residences and create a 'resident' status that would authorize a person to acquire property in certain municipalities only after they have lived there for a year. But will these measures be enough?

These dynamics are driven by a profound change in the lifestyle of the most well-off people; those who, particularly since the Covid crisis and the development of working from home, are buying secondary residences on the outskirts of large cities. This famous 'world after Covid' celebrated by the media, is generating an invisible social violence: that of the exclusion of the least well-off from their places of life and birth. As usual, the exclusion of the ordinary majority is justified by the rhetoric of the invisible hand of the market, of first-come-first-served. The argument is always the same: the rich support life in these regions thanks to the trickle-down effect they induce. This theory, previously used to justify metropolitanization on the pretext that the winning territories indirectly redistributed part of their wealth to the losing territories, exonerates the upper classes from the impact of their decision to purchase residences in coastal areas.

This language gets used by certain elected officials with the aim of justifying the economy-boosting gentrification of the coastal areas. While there is no doubt that the construction of residences and the arrival of wealthy families promote the local economy, this material observation obscures an essential dimension, namely, where are the less well-off going to live? How are we to measure the resentment sometimes caused when a person can no longer live where he or she was born?

In February 2022, at a hearing devoted to land speculation in Corsica, the nationalist MP Jean-Félix Acquaviva mentioned this cultural dimension, one that does not show up in the surveys of local economic statistics:

> If the trend in construction of secondary residences continues as we have seen over the last two decades in Corsica, if it contin-

ues in terms of the level of poverty among Corsicans, if we let it happen that the latter increasingly become foreigners on their own land, we won't be able to say tomorrow that we weren't warned. The situation into which we are gradually letting the island slip may well create a major headache for our people, the Corsican people, who no longer have enough room in their own country. Do we want the islanders to have no choice but that of leaving, being dispossessed, or living on reserves like North American Indians? Do we really want to send the signal that democracy and the law are powerless? For a Corsican, land is not only an economic asset, it is a fundamental element of the identity of a people.[13]

Some months later, in July, the FLNC claimed responsibility for the bombing of sixteen secondary residences. In a press release, the clandestine organization denounced what it viewed as the deliberate murder of the Corsican people.

In a general context where the stock of moderately priced housing is shrinking like nobody's business, where real-estate prices in certain coastal areas have soared to Parisian prices, and where the majority of secondary residence stock belongs to the upper social categories (and in particular to the ten per cent of the wealthiest households in the country), many elected officials believe, like the mayor of Saint-Lunaire in Ille-et-Vilaine, that 'we've reached a stage where there's going to be a confrontation'.[14]

Everywhere, the dual impact of gentrification and airbnb-ization is causing an explosion in prices and, automatically, a refocusing on short and expensive stays. In these gentrified spaces, five-star campsites are spreading, while the number of one- or two-star campsites is decreasing. Camping, a traditional form of tourist accommodation for the working classes, is seeing its prices soar and its clientele change. Welcome to bourgeois camping, and even glamping! This form of cultural appropriation is always the last stage of gentrification. It recalls the appropriation of working-class brands by the bourgeoisie of the big cities: individual neighbourhoods, cafes and even football stadiums, all those emblematic places of working-class culture, have retained their appearances, but ordinary people are definitively excluded from them.

So, something is changing on the coasts. From the surge in the price of housing per square metre that prevents the working classes from accessing property to the rise in the price of summer accommodation, the coasts have once again become enclosed spaces on a closed sea. The main or secondary residences of wealthy retirees or senior executives are spreading. Everywhere, the Côte-d'Azurization of the coast is underway and will inevitably lead to the eviction of the working classes.

Of course, no one is stopping paid holidays or access to the coast, and the less well-off classes can still go to the beach; but something is happening, a symbolic return to square one. If the 1986 'law on coasts' that regulates the development of the coastline still allows free access to the seaside, it will not stop the steamroller of gentrification. The coasts have always attracted the bourgeoisie, but today the pressure on real estate is the result of a numerically much larger group. This very large group of active or retired upper classes represents nearly 20–25 per cent of the population, a demographic weight heavy enough to cause irreversible sociological changes on territories much larger than those of a neighbourhood or a village. Here lies the paradox of this inegalitarian model: it works! Indeed, this model has continued to create wealth that benefits a considerable fraction of the population – but at the cost of weakening the ordinary majority.

We cannot understand the gentrification of territory without setting it within the sociological context of the disappearance of a middle class that was previously the majority. In the last century, the gentrification of Cap Ferret, Antibes or the Left Bank districts of Paris did not impact on the life of a middle class that was perfectly integrated, economically and culturally. But, today, the gentrification of the coastlines and all the areas of mainland France obviously does not have the same meaning, at a time when the middle class has imploded in a twofold movement. As economist Branko Milanović explains, globalization has caused a fraction of the middle class to aspire upwards and entailed a collapse of the majority towards the bottom.[15] In this 'hourglass' organization, the Western middle class is disappearing to make way for two antagonistic poles: upper social categories that monopolize the bulk of high incomes, and an ordinary majority that is becoming increasingly fragile. Thanks to their unprecedented demographic weight, the upper strata[16] are able to reshape not only the media, and the political and cultural landscape, but also the social geography of Western countries.

Real-estate specialists are used to contrasting 'tense zones' (*zones tendues* with high demand on housing and rising prices per square metre) and 'relaxed zones' (*zones détendues* with less demand, and stable or even falling prices per square metre). Behind this technical semantics lies a more prosaic reality: the so-called tense zones correspond to the territories desired by the upper classes. The real-estate market is therefore driven by these categories and their residential choices. These choices determine the future of the various territories but also, in a ripple effect, the public policies (in particular the construction of social housing) that will be brought in as a marginal response to this juggernaut.

The gentrification of the coasts restricts the locals' access to housing, but it also impacts on the less well-off holidaymakers. To continue being able to go on holiday, they are forced to change their habits: to travel less far, to travel for shorter periods, or even to stop travelling. Twenty years ago, two-thirds of French people said they went on holiday. In 2019, this proportion fell to 58 per cent. While 82 per cent of senior executives go on holiday, only 47 per cent of workers do so. In 1999, 47 per cent of people with incomes below

€1,200 went on holiday, and this proportion fell to 37 per cent in 2019.[17] As prices per square metre rise, the entire social landscape is changing, gradually depriving ordinary people of anywhere to go. The proliferation of 'high-end' real-estate projects and even of beachside gated communities[18] gives us an indication of the future that awaits the least well-off in these territories.

The sea is in perpetual motion, and so is the place of ordinary people in society.

In Antiquity, the Greeks and Romans saw the sea as a space reserved for the gods. The nineteenth-century bourgeoisie made it a holiday destination. After a short period of democratization, the 'woke', trendy middle classes of the new millennium are banking on the law of the market to make it their closed playground once again. From yesterday's seaside bathing to today's gentrification, we are discreetly returning to square one. On the surface, nothing has changed: the appearances remain more or less the same, but the fisherman's house has become a dwelling for the Parisian executive. This shift is reminiscent of that of large cities, in which apartments and artisan spaces in working-class neighbourhoods are being transformed into lofts, and have not housed a worker for several decades.

This step backwards has taken place quietly, and even in cheerful good humour. The fact that a young person from a modest background can no longer live where he or she was born (the working-class neighbourhoods of large cities, or coastal areas) does not bother many people.

Let's be clear, there's no 'land grab' going on. In reality, in their usual manner, the new trendy bourgeoisie does not drive people out or impose itself by force: it has no need to do so. It simply follows, almost unwittingly, the invisible hand of the real-estate market. Or rather, just like yesterday, when it fetched up in the working-class neighbourhoods of large cities, it now explains that it is allowing the spaces it is moving into to improve, to regain economic dynamism, to create local jobs. A little mood music in the media is also used to justify this dynamic, suggesting that this movement is consistent with the need to 'get away from the city', to work from home, developing co-residences for the good of the natives. A perfect world, in other words.

Given the increase in the gap between regional average incomes and real-estate prices, we can now acknowledge that plans are afoot to end working-class holidays at the seaside. Sociologically, and in the medium term, the Atlantic coast will resemble the sociology of gentrified neighbourhoods in cities; the urban upper classes, the traditional or progressive bourgeoisie, and wealthy retirees. The decline in mobility is part of this gentrification process, so we can safely predict that a process of gentrification and ageing across all coastlines will become the norm. As in the metropolises, local elected officials – aware that these territories cannot live without workers, especially 'key workers' – are seeking to counter the process by creating social housing, but this homeopathic policy seems a rather derisory way of regulating market forces. The construction of such social housing is unable to compensate for the disappearance of an affordable private sector,[19] the only sector likely to remain within the reach of a significant number of the less well-off. The supply of housing intended for them will gradually be reduced to social housing, and the vast majority of the working classes will disperse to the peri-urban or rural peripheries. As in the 1980s, gentrification is described positively by urban elites and opinion leaders (who are often major players in this gentrification).[20] This overarching vision highlights the benefits generated by the arrival of new residents who are more demanding about their living environment, the provision of services and commercial goods and who, by their very presence, generate activity and employment – for the least well-off. The media strongly promoted this narrative during the Covid crisis, which saw a large part of the population consider moving and/or buying a secondary residence, if possible by the sea.

But basically, what is striking in these representations is the perception of peripheral France as a playground, a *terra incognita* inhabited by natives anxiously and impatiently awaiting the arrival of their saviours who, thanks to the trickle-down effect of their income (salaries and retirement pensions), will revive struggling employment areas. This fairy-tale, which leaves aside the question of the relevance of the economic model, helps to justify the quiet secession of the upper classes and the erection of invisible walls between the top and the bottom strata.

The 'unbowed' bourgeoisie[21] and the sense of heritage

The groups that denounce the gentrification of the coasts have an air of *déjà vu*, of over-familiarity. When Bretons demonstrate,[22] proclaiming that 'Brittany is not a secondary residence!', they are echoing the people of Barcelona, who unfurl banners stating 'Barcelona is not for sale'.[23] In this metropolis, demonstrations against gentrification, mass tourism and the privatization of public spaces have been recurring for decades now. Leading actions against land speculation, Breton and Barcelona activists demonstrate against the same surge in real-estate prices, but also against the same tourism industry. The denunciation of secondary residences that are left deserted all year round echoes the denunciation of empty apartments that are used only for speculation. In both cases, they highlight the fact that young people and the working classes no longer have the means to access these spaces and the employment concentrated in them. From London to Berlin, activists have continued to perpetrate sometimes astonishing actions, such as the attack on a cereal bar in the Shoreditch district, 'the symbol of the gentrification of a district, the rise in rents and the departure of the least well-off households'.[24] But it is clear that these demonstrations have had only a derisory impact on the social evolution of metropolises. They failed mainly because they didn't mobilize strongly enough. Indeed, strangely enough, these demonstrations, despite taking place in the electoral strongholds of the left and the far-left (the bourgeois neighbourhoods of large cities), have never mobilized local residents – despite their avowed sensitivity to social questions.

The 'unbowed' bourgeoisie that populates these neighbourhoods has not joined the protesters. Although it waxes very eloquent on the issue of inequalities, the denunciation of the One Per Cent, capitalism, and social injustice, it rarely leaves its lofts to swell the ranks of the demonstrators. But perhaps this new 'rebellious and progressive' bourgeoisie does not really want to draw attention to how much it has gained from the very capitalism it is always denouncing? Perhaps it does not really want us to talk about the fantastic leg-up it has achieved, thanks to the increase in the price of land, nor the heritage it has built up, thanks to the market?

Indeed, how can we imagine that beneficiaries of this model would raise their voices in protest in the metropolises and on the coasts? Twenty years ago, we noted that, for these reasons, no serious social movement would come from the big cities, not even from the suburbs, which have so far only produced riots – that is to say, destruction and violence – easily contained by throwing money around. For decades, as in all Western countries, anger has come from elsewhere. Far from the coasts, far from the metropolises, where the majority of the working classes now live, it is peripheral France[25] that has been the scene of one of the most important social movements since the Popular Front.

2

The forbidden city

In 2018, it was a coastal *département*, the Gironde, which was at the heart of the Yellow Vest movement. Bordeaux stood out for the size of the marches there and the increase in blockades around the city. The intensity of the demonstrations in this *département* would reveal to local and national elites that 'quiet metropolitanization' does not exist, that people's lives cannot be organized on the sole basis of spreadsheets setting out the economic performance of a few sectors. Clearly, the speed and intensity of the two processes of metropolitanization and gentrification had created the conditions for a major storm. Historian Pierre Vermeren notes that the *département* gained 400,000 inhabitants in thirty years (a third of its population) and that Bordeaux has become the most attractive metropolis in France:

> The data are quite simple, and to be frank, inevitable. Bordeaux absorbed only 10% of the growth in the *département*'s population (nearly 40,000 inhabitants); the Bordeaux metropolitan area as a whole absorbed half (nearly 200,000). Rural Gironde and the Gironde of small towns, which still represents nearly one in two Girondins, absorbed the other half [. . .]. The renovation

of the city, the considerable investments made in its development, and the associated communication operations, have tripled the price of real estate, which is now close to Parisian prices in the most exclusive districts. The euphoria in Bordeaux is very largely linked to this speculative surge, one of the most lasting and most massive effects of which has been to drive out the original working and middle classes from the city centre and, by a ripple effect, from the nearest towns, or at least from their most prominent districts [. . .]. The median salary in the Gironde, which is close to that of France at €1,600 per month, has inevitably led to the departure of the working-class populations, artisans, employees and junior and medium-ranking civil servants who keep the agglomeration running, in particular the city centre. However, with nearly 400 construction sites in 2018, the Bordeaux agglomeration is a huge employment pool for workers, artisans and building earthmovers. The big increase in retired baby-boomers and the enormous University Hospital Centre that resulted from it (the largest employer in the agglomeration), combined with the expansion of tourism, have resulted in an explosion of low-skilled jobs in catering, hotels, health, and personal services. Workplace and home are therefore separate for the majority of people – often dozens of kilometres apart. Bordeaux now has twice as many executives as resident workers.[1]

In just a few years, therefore, the *département* has experienced an economic and social restructuring that other metropolitan areas had taken half a century to achieve. The process has automatically given rise to an inegalitarian organization, split between its large gentrified city, in which the presence of working-class categories is limited to social housing neighbourhoods, and its working-class peripheries. The upper classes choose the city centre, the closest of the peripheries and the coasts, while the less well-off and working-class categories fall back on the peripheral Gironde. These spaces of the 'subjected peri-urban' zone, as the geographer Laurent Chalard calls it,[2] thus primarily accommodate employees and workers who, in order to access property, have been forced to move away from the heart of the Bordeaux metropolis to municipalities where the price of land is much lower (Médoc, Cubzaguais, Blayais). The geographer notes that these spaces, where households have few means but are dependent on cars, have been the bastions of the Yellow Vests mobilization. They are also those where the National Rally vote is taking root (as in the last presidential and then legislative elections of 2022).

The model produces the same effects everywhere: the same relegation and the same invisible social violence. By moving away from the most active employment areas, from the territories that count economically and culturally, the ordinary majority is gradually seeing its social horizon, and that of its children, shrink.

In Bordeaux, as in all metropolises, elected officials think they are generating and managing the dazzling development of their city. In truth, they are generating and managing nothing: it is the market that is in control. They still pride themselves on their results. Unable to lead the movement, they pretend to have initiated it. They are merely the puppets of a powerful economic, financial, and real-estate dynamic, within which the members of the political sphere act as dumb waiters.

Urban renovation and restructuring operations, green developments, and the upgrading of amenities make it possible to publicize the objective improvement in living conditions. The reality is that these areas, integrated into the global economy, attract companies from the tertiary economy, research, logistics and construction (plus the automatic concentration of head offices, administrations and universities); this dynamic is therefore less driven by public policies than by the law of supply and demand.

However much local officials boast of their success, they are only the playthings of the market. In reality, any idiot can 'run' a big city, since he or she is not the pilot, but at best the co-pilot. However, the paradox is that, these days, we see all the political big shots, the stars of the technostructure, jostling to run a metropolis (a territory that functions all by itself), while human and intellectual needs and resources are mainly located in the areas in difficulty, the deindustrialized and deprived zones of peripheral France. How can we take seriously those political elites who fight to represent the territories where the 'political sphere' has been erased in favour of the market, while refusing to serve the territories where, conversely, expectations of public policies are at their highest?

Urban cloning

In order to be persuaded of the primacy of the market over politics, one only has to observe what the large Western metropolises have become. From New York to Paris, from Milan to Lyon, from London to Bordeaux, the architecture of the new buildings, the commercial and cultural provision, the green developments, and the levels of communication are absolutely identical.

In all latitudes, metropolises increasingly resemble the village in *The Prisoner*.[3] These cloned villages form an archipelago[4] where people think and vote more or less identically. This world is one of reproduction, of conformism – not one of creation, and even less one of subversion. Moving from metropolis to metropolis now resembles an immobile journey. This is the paradox: these places that sell themselves as representative of 'hypermobility' have become places of stagnation, of confinement, of repetition, of cultural and intellectual stagnation.

The media and experts often speak of the counter-society, referring to the tendency of certain working-class categories to fall back on a narrow sense of identity or community, but this denunciation ignores the real counter-society that has been built up since the 1980s as a result of the secession of the elites, the upper classes and the winners of globalization. The metropolis and its dependencies are the embodiment of this: a social enclave (*entre-soi*), implying homogenization and social reproduction, a concentration of wealth and jobs,[5] aloofness, and the abandonment of the common good.

Everywhere, these barbaric metropolises[6] give birth to the same evils, the same tensions, the same inequalities. With the exception of social housing neighbourhoods, the working classes have been eliminated from all spaces, including football stadiums, where their presence is now tolerated only in the cheaper seats. The social geography of these sports arenas is almost a metaphor for the ideal society of elites: a majority of comfortably seated upper classes and a minority of modest classes penned in and kept under control in one or two stands. A gentrified city and the poor in social housing neighbourhoods. The dream.

The cemetery of the political left

For half a century, the entire French technostructure has wagered on metropolization. Oddly enough, the emergence of this inegalitarian urban model has not been debated in France. One explanation lies in the communicational and especially political promotion of this liberal model, one that lies at the heart of our old French republican and egalitarian system. The right could not directly challenge this model, the liberals even less so. An inegalitarian policy imposed by the right would inevitably have provoked a violent social reaction. The stroke of genius was to entrust this work to the camp of social progress, of the defence of the working classes, of the so-called progressive left, supported by the new urban bourgeoisie.

Metropolitanization is merely a business, a gigantic business governed by the law of the market alone; the worst of capitalism, equipped with the best communications agency, i.e. the left.

Everything was present in embryo from the beginning of the 1980s, when the left made its famous liberal shift. This abandonment of the social issue, and ultimately of the working classes, was achieved in stages, with certain events contributing to it. The first urban riots in the Lyon metropolitan area would offer the left the opportunity to justify its ideological adaptation. The replacement of societal questions by the social question would be carried out in the name of anti-racism and the defence of minorities.[7] This shift announced the adaptation of the socialist narrative, not to society, but to the economic and societal dynamics of large cities. Through successive shifts, the left would adapt its discourse to the quintessence of the neoliberal model emerging in the metropolises. This development, which sealed the ideological alliance between economic liberalism and cultural liberalism,[8] announced the coming victories of the socialists and then the environmentalists in those bastions of capital previously held by the right. In this regard, we can never overemphasize the importance of Bertrand Delanoë's election in 2001 in Paris, the richest metropolis in France, at the very moment when the working classes were being cheerfully forced out by the agents of gentrification, the notorious 'bobos' or 'bourgeois bohemians'. It was by capturing this new electorate, this new trendy bourgeoisie, that the left would win Paris.[9] But winning Paris obviously meant losing the people. The successive victories of the left in all the metropolitan cities announced the ideological and then political confinement of the working class. Now a prisoner of its metropolitan ghetto, the left was definitively cutting itself off from its traditional sociological base in peripheral France.

Metropolitanization would prove to be its graveyard. Relying on the steamroller of the market and an emphasis on communications (the 'open', 'solidary', 'green' city), the metropolitan model has now imposed itself in all regions, entailing the same social and environmental devastation everywhere.

However, in recent years, reinforced by the protest emanating from the inhabitants and elected officials of peripheral France, criticism of metropolitanization is increasing. The model is less and less attractive, even for those who live there, who are now expressing their desire to leave the big cities. Surprised and weakened by the Yellow Vests, the government has to some extent given in and launched 'rebalancing' policies towards small and medium-sized towns. But these operations are more of a PR stunt than a matter of substantial policies. In fact, the metropolises still monopolize the bulk of public investment. For the record, the 'Action Cœur de Ville Programme' budget for the revitalization of 200[10] cities is around five billion euros over five years, while that of Greater Paris alone exceeds forty billion. A 'crazy amount of cash'![11]

Having bought into the benefits of free trade and competition between territories, the ruling class will not change course. So, how can social and cultural separatism be combated by relying on the economic, societal and territorial model that is its source? This headlong rush, this laissez-faire, these policies that create all the evils that the system claims to combat (deindustrialization, precariousness, inequality) are gradually depriving the ordinary majority of residents of any prospects. After the parenthesis of the *Trente Glorieuses*, the dominant and upper classes decided to close shop. But in silence. And, if possible, by pretending that the shop was still open.

It's a bit like in the cover-up operations launched by certain small towns where the windows of closed shops are covered with *trompe l'oeil* designs: here, a flowery poster 'replaces' the florist, there an image of a library 'replaces' a bookshop.

In the meantime, the metropolises are completing the task of getting rid of the working classes by continuing to communicate about their openness. The last step is to impose a new local tax on consumption – to 'protect the environment'.

The forbidden city

In 2023, petrol-run vehicles registered before 1 January 2006, and diesel engines registered before 1 January 2011, were banned from driving in Greater Paris. Following suit, the major French cities planned to gradually ban the oldest vehicles from their streets. Lyon, Nice, Toulouse, Montpellier, Strasbourg, Rouen, Marseille . . . no metropolis would fail to respond to the call.

In 2025, around fifty of them will have their own LEZ (low-emission zone). In most European metropolises, these restrictions are already in effect. We are thinking in particular of London, which has reestablished this vehicle tax for years, setting up an urban toll at its borders for the most heavily polluting cars, and Brussels, which has opted for the payment of a flat rate online. In the same way that the gentrification of working-class neighbourhoods was presented as an improvement in housing, these restrictive measures are being deployed in the name of combating pollution. The Île-de-France health observatory indicates in particular that the establishment of a LEZ would prevent eighty deaths per year in the region (that's a precise figure!) and generally combat childhood asthma. For environmental and health reasons, it will therefore be necessary to have a newish car in the future if you want to access the centres of the metropolises.

This policy is likely to accelerate, since it is estimated that, in three years, twelve million motorists will be forced to replace their heavily polluting vehicles. Despite government aid, these new acquisitions (in particular for electric vehicles, the price of which remains very high, in a context of lack of supply on the second-hand market) will remain out of reach of the poorer categories.

This 'green' policy has never ceased to go hand in hand with the process of social restructuring. Moreover, the 'car-free day' (which carried the seeds of the development of LEZs) was born in the 1990s, at a time when the eviction of the working classes was gaining momentum. Then, it was apparently just about having a positive impact on the environment, the quality of life and health. Things accelerated at the beginning of the 2000s, when the new bourgeoisie seized political power in the big cities.

After all, this policy responds to a real concern of the upper classes, who constantly complain about the quality of the air, noise pollution and traffic jams caused by people who do not live there. These demands are therefore consistent with a population that overwhelmingly supports the development of clean (so-called 'soft') mobility: electric cars, if possible as part of a car-share scheme, bicycles and scooters. This eco-village spirit is also very favourable to the increase in the price of real-estate assets, a secondary benefit that is far from negligible and keeps the least well-off at a distance, without having to express this aim or to take responsibility for it. The logical outcome of this spirit is this return to a consumption tax at the border of the 'open cities'. This model, which excludes 'those who drive diesel' (mostly the working classes) and will soon exclude 'those who smoke ciggies'[12] (tobacco consumption is increasingly a social marker: in twenty years, while the share of daily smokers has dropped from 28 per cent to eighteen per cent in the upper categories, it has not decreased in the less well-off categories, stagnating at thirty per cent), is the model of the city without the people.

From the Atlantic Wall to the walls of the citadel city, the landscape of the working classes has radically changed. This does not only raise the question of money but also the more fundamental one of a change in life prospects. From now on, the horizon is blocked for the majority of the working classes who live on the other side of the walls, out in peripheral France.

The sealing off of the 'city' by new invisible borders impacts working-class society at a level that goes beyond the social trend charts of the French finance ministry. Symbolically, the 'city' is also less and less frequented by ordinary people, who are deserting elections, trade unions, political parties, and even voluntary associations.¹³ These places of democratic life are now kept going by the most highly integrated categories, built around them and for them. It is they who benefit from the model – whatever party is in power.

This forbidden city has become the place of networking, where social reproduction is the norm,¹⁴ where education no longer plays its role of social emancipation, where the *grandes écoles* seem to have erased all trace of students from working-class backgrounds.¹⁵ It's a society where young people from working-class backgrounds are gradually getting used to the idea that this world is not for them. Prospects for the working classes and young people from these backgrounds are getting dimmer and dimmer; this is the observation that we have been hammering home for twenty years¹⁶ by showing that now, for equal social categories, the mobility of young people from working-class backgrounds is lower in peripheral France than in the metropolises.¹⁷ This is a reality that, despite the mobilization of a few elected officials or associations, is struggling to make itself visible.

However, the figures are irrefutable. The chances of social advancement for individuals from working-class backgrounds (i.e. children of workers and employees) vary widely, depending on the territory of birth. Apparently, it is in the Île-de-France that the social advancement of the working classes is the strongest. In Seine-Saint-Denis, social mobility is over forty per cent, while in Indre or Creuse it does not reach 25 per cent.¹⁸ In 2022, another report once again confirmed this evidence: the chances of social advancement are greater when you live in a working-class neighbourhood in the metropolis (near a dynamic job market and a plethora of educational options) than in a rural or industrial area of peripheral France.¹⁹ This INSEE note also specifies that

> those who are most likely to improve their income compared to that of their parents are more likely to be men, residents of

Île-de-France, and of course those whose parents have a higher degree. Above all, it appears that the children of immigrants have a higher than average upward mobility and that upward mobility is identical (19%) in Seine-Saint-Denis and in the wealthy *département* of Hauts-de-Seine.

None of this is very new, since it has been clear for decades that the sensitive neighbourhoods of large cities produce a 'middle class'[20] population of invisible households, who leave these neighbourhoods in their phase of upward mobility. This dynamic is all the more remarkable because it developed at a time when the decline of the middle class was becoming widespread. All these dynamics have already been analysed by English-language observers, in particular the British, who have been warning for years about the deterioration of access to university for young white people from the working class who live in the peripheral UK.[21] In France, these themes are beginning to emerge[22] but always come up against the difficulty of a social and geographical representation that turns its back on this working-class France. As gentrification spreads, the mobility of young people, as well as that of workers in peripheral France, is now confronted with the obstacle of the high cost and scarcity of housing in large cities. Far from the myth of mobility for all, we are on the contrary witnessing a form of forced sedentarization, which in fact accentuates the decline in mobility and, above all, the impression that society is closing its doors.

This lack of prospects is leading many households today to abandon the idea of finding a stable job or, for some young people, to give up the idea of studying. Many of them consider that 'university is too difficult for me, I'd never dare leave my village to follow a training in craftsmanship – that's my dream – or Sciences Po. It's not for children from the countryside.'[23] For their part, the *grandes écoles*, like the metropolises in which they are located, are continuing their process of top-down social homogenization. The subject raised by these dynamics invisible to the upper strata and destructive for the lower ones goes beyond the mere question of social mobility. Reducing the future of working-class youth to a simple automatic system of downward or upward mobility is typical of an exclusively technocratic approach. Modelling the fate of ordinary people to an elevator (or a descender) is part of a process of denying the richness of ordinary life. This dehumanized representation of the working-class bloc misses the point: the question is not primarily about going up or down, but about living decently, that is to say, being culturally respected, including by moving around in one's environment.

This reduction of ordinary life to a 'technical' problem (the size and power of the social elevator) not only evades the overall question of the place of the working classes in society but also diverts attention from the responsibility of the upper classes (precisely those who wax eloquent about the state of the elevator) in creating a model that excludes people.

This sidelining, this displacement from the centre to the economic and cultural peripheries constitutes the heart of the social and cultural violence suffered by the working classes – a violence whose perpetrators are never identified.

3

The social imprint

The gap between facts and their representations has rarely been so striking: the upper strata are withdrawing into their citadel, but promoting an inclusive society. Their members tell us that the purchasing power of ordinary people is increasing, even though their incomes are stagnating or declining. They claim to be fighting for public services and the social model, while seeking to dismantle it. They advocate equality, while promoting an inegalitarian model. And so on. This communication of an inverted reality prevents us from going back to the source and identifying those who make this shift possible.

Indeed, this radical transformation of society does not seem to be driven by any actor, any person in charge. If, rightly, the ultra-rich and multinationals are sometimes identified, an embarrassed silence surrounds all those who make this movement possible, even if they did not necessarily initiate it: the upper social categories. For the first time, the working classes are facing a new bourgeoisie that takes responsibility neither for its class position nor for the effects of the project it supports. Imbued with the liberal and consumerist individualism of the times, practising for decades a discreet selection in matters of housing and education, the upper classes are most often unaware of taking part in a real process of secession. Indifferent to the fate of an ordinary majority with whom they no longer rub shoulders, morally comforted by the adherence to a vague progressivism, they perceive their political, economic and residential choices as at best positive, and at worst as neutral for society and the less well-off. Withdrawn behind invisible walls, the trendy, benevolent bourgeoisie may not have sought the effects of the model, but it endorses that model. In reality, it is in fact jointly responsible for a social outcome that it is perfectly easy to measure, but which does not give rise to any debate, to any televised chatter.

Discretion is not, however, what characterizes this new bourgeoisie. The winners of the globalized model express themselves everywhere and all the time on continuous news channels, on movie screens, on social networks. They talk, talk, talk about everything, about the end of the world, the world after the end of the world, geopolitics, living together, democracy, fascism, mushroom picking, euthanasia, the future of the left, the right, the centre . . . This background noise never stops, and feeds on itself 24 hours a day.

This flow of words and images occasionally allows the working classes to appear, in the best case as grotesque figures on the way to disappearing, in the worst case as deplorable representatives of hatred.

The whole show is controlled by the new bourgeoisie, from the sets to the staging to the casting, in which, moreover, it reserves the best roles for itself. Overplaying the posture of the 'progressive' person concerned with the fate of humanity, the trendy bourgeois regularly talk about the need to change a model that they never cease to promote. Consumption, mobility, inequalities . . . 'The time for change is now', they say.[1] But the area in which these hypocrites excel is the environment. And, to add an extra sheen to their green communication, they can rely on figures. In this area, everything is measured, framed, neatly marked out, with trends clearly identified.

Ecologically responsible, socially irresponsible

Statistics are a symptom of technocratic drift, and now set the agenda for any debate. They condition politics. No local elected official would risk initiating the slightest public policy today without a trend chart, most often produced by experts, sometimes Lysenkos,[2] who are very far removed from the territories they are analysing. Today, modelling is less an aid to decision-making than a way of homogenizing thought.

It is within this numerical framework that the uniformized discourse of the woke, green middle classes now finds its cosy little niche. This is how the 'ecological footprint' was born – a footprint that allows one to measure scientifically the pressure exerted by the population on nature. Indeed, this tool calculates the quantity of natural resources consumed by different countries, people, communities and companies. It is supplemented by the 'carbon footprint', that is to say the quantity of carbon emitted by a country, a person, a community, or a company by its consumption of energy and raw materials. Armed with these indicators, the ruling and upper classes can warn of the ecological catastrophe that is coming (that is already here). If, basically, we need to underline their contradictory posture of referring to the need to change our way of life, while refusing to question the globalized model that favours the main sources of ecological disaster (free trade, the maritime movement of everyday consumer goods, the huge growth in air traffic, and international tourism), we must welcome their desire to question the state of the environment.

But, at a time when every area of life seems to be measured, when the impact of each individual is followed step by step, there is still a permanent blind spot that escapes modelling, and yet is essential, since it concerns the functioning of society as a whole: that of the social impact of the bourgeoisie. If the upper classes have been won over to the idea of the damage they can cause to the environment, they seem, on the other hand, foreign to the idea of their social responsibility. Environmental responsibility is everywhere, at school, at the cinema, in the business world, at the supermarket. Social responsibility is nowhere.

To address this shortcoming, might it not be time to create a 'socio-responsible' label? Based on the model of the 'eco-responsible' label, which identifies the products and services that treat the planet with the most respect, the socio-label could be granted to political, economic, societal or residential choices.

Why not have one socio-label that would assess the impact of an economic decision on the employment of the working classes? Another that would assess the impact of deregulation on industrial employment? Yet another that would assess the impact of buying real estate in a tense zone, where housing supply is inaccessible to the poorest? And a last one that would assess the consequences of the upper classes choosing private education for the educational destiny of the poorest?

There is no shortage of issues to tackle. Beyond its practical interest, this public-health measure would perhaps make it possible to make the upper classes feel a sense of responsibility: they are always ready to denounce the ultra-rich, the CAC 40 stock market index, and even – when they are feeling particularly bold – international finance,[3] but they have far less to say about their own influence.

We rightly denounce the destruction of the environment; is it not time to measure the social destruction of ordinary society? To finally draw up an accurate social and societal assessment of the upper classes? Today, this assessment is incomplete and opaque. Following the model of large companies, these upper categories have made it illegible by erasing their social footprint. Indeed, to divert attention from their responsibilities, they accuse 'the system' and its 'inequalities' and designate a culprit everyone can agree on: the one per cent.

The ad nauseam denunciation of this one per cent is today the *sole* way the bourgeoisie shows any fight. Subversive and radical, it mobilizes, like Bill Gates, to denounce the 'one per cent of the rich who own forty per cent of the wealth'[4] and the scandal of the ten largest fortunes in the world (estimated at 1,500 billion dollars). Here's a rhetorical question: who doesn't find that scandalous? In reality, this one per cent allows the upper classes to include themselves in the mass of the exploited.

The so-called progressive bourgeoisie, an expert in the facile denunciation of the rich, never sees itself at the 'top'. Fully opposed to power, it protects itself by blending into the mass, that of the 99 per cent.[5] Refusing to acknowledge its class position, it stages a fictitious class struggle that pits the 99 per cent against the one per cent. The 'united class' of the 99 per cent brings together individuals on the poverty line (€885 for a single person), and the working classes, the unemployed as well as those with jobs, workers as well as executives. In this immense conglomerate, everyone is a victim, no one is responsible, except the ultra-rich. But, in this consensual mishmash, an essential question is never asked: who makes this one per cent possible? Who makes the permanence of the model possible? Unless we consider that 'the one per cent' is the majority (which, I'm sure you will agree, would be completely absurd), it is difficult to understand how such a small part of the population manages to impose its model and even indeed to win elections.

A quick glance at the income scale or household wealth[6] in France will quickly dispel the myth of the 99 per cent. While there are losers and winners, the latter are not only the 'ultra-rich' but all the upper categories. Analysing monthly income for the equivalent of a person after taxes and social benefits (what is called the standard of living) shows where the one per cent stand. In 2018, the richest one per cent of French had €6,651 per month, the richest five per cent had €4,090 and the richest ten per cent had €3,261. The wealth threshold (double the median income) is €3,542. This means that half of the French population has less than €1,771 per month. If we look at another scale, that of salaries, the top twenty per cent earn more than €3,000 per month. When upper classes denounce the one per cent, they are pointing their fingers at each other. In other words, the Torquemadas of the one per cent who saturate the media space are statistically 'rich'. In reality, and without confusing these upper classes with the billionaires of Silicon Valley, there is indeed a social group that benefits from the model (20–25% of the population) and a weakened majority bloc, identified for half a century by most social indicators.

Thus, when we speak 'in general' of unemployment, precariousness or poverty, we are in fact speaking first of the unemployment, precariousness and poverty of workers and employees. In 2019, when 3.5 per cent of senior executives were affected by unemployment, this rate rose to 9.2 per cent for employees, 9.3 per cent for skilled workers and 17.7 per cent for specialized workers. Similarly, when we talk about precarious jobs, we are again talking about employees and workers whose rate of precariousness reached 17.1 and 21.9 per cent respectively in 2019, compared to 6.5 per cent for senior executives.

All too glad to blur class distinctions, the upper classes know how to choose their side when it comes to deciding on major political directions. From the Treaty of Maastricht to joining Macronism via the referendum on the European Constitution in 2005, they always vote for the dominant model. A model that, of course, allows the rich to be ever richer, but which also allows them to stand out from the crowd, as evidenced by their wealth, often originally acquired for next to nothing and enhanced by the gentrification of urban areas (main residences) and coastal areas (secondary residences).

The acquisition and growth of this wealth is all the more remarkable because it occurred at a time when the middle and working classes were becoming more fragile. The 'upper' strata have wasted no time. In less than half a century of deregulation, in the shadow of the ultra-rich, the new bourgeoisie has caught up with the old. The value of apartments, lofts and other individual residences acquired in the old working-class neighbourhoods is now on a par with that of private mansions. While this wealth is less ostentatious than that of the traditional bourgeoisie, it has nothing to do with castles in the air.

In 2018, the median net worth[7] (debts deducted) was €117,000; this means that half of French households own less than this amount and the other half own more. This average already makes it possible to 'place' homeowners in all major French cities and more generally the upper classes. It is estimated that the median wealth of senior executive households is €219,000 (as opposed to €37,500 for workers, €25,300 for employees and €12,300 for unskilled workers). In other words, the upper classes thus have a median net worth nine times higher than that of employees.[8] These happy property owners can now supplement their income by renting out their main or secondary residences via Airbnb. Let us recall here that if the increase in secondary residences destabilizes the housing supply of the least well-off, it contributes to a significant improvement in the income of the most well-off households, who currently hold more than 34 per cent of the total. Their enemy may be finance, but it is certainly not wealth! Thirty years of metropolitanization (and therefore globalization and financialization) have allowed these upper classes to build up a wealth inaccessible to the ordinary majority.

Quietly, the upper classes are winning on all counts. Overplaying the progressive stance, denying its dominant social position, the bourgeoisie does not feel responsible for the social effects of the model it endorses. In the same way that its facade of environmentalism makes us forget the ecological impact of its way of life,[9] the display of its openness to others and its fight for a more inclusive society makes it possible to conceal its social impact.

All these issues actually share the same ambiguity. The upper classes are imposing an inegalitarian model while being offended by the wealth of the ultra-rich, imposing a multicultural society while protecting themselves from diversity (a model in which they absolutely do not believe, as shown by their residential and educational selectivity), and putting forward a radical environmentalism (but continuing to favour metropolitanization and destructive globalized free trade).

The peril of social distancing

But deep down, there is a common thread: the refusal of social otherness and an indifference to the fate of ordinary people. This indifference, the culmination of the whole process, is characteristic of a social group that no longer plays a part in class conflict. In this world, the conflict between the dominant classes (the bourgeoisie) and the dominated classes (the working classes) no longer has any reason to exist, since they no longer rub shoulders, and no longer even set eyes on each other.

This social abstinence on the part of the upper strata, which leads to the reduction of any intellectual, cultural or physical contact with the ordinary majority, has created geographical and cognitive bubbles in which social enclaves and social reproduction are now the norm. In this perfect world where its social, cultural and political security seem assured, the bourgeoisie no longer even needs to oppose the working classes.

Today, it is the distancing of the 'other' that ensures social order. In this society, which is not a real society, the working classes are not enemies, they are just forgotten. The new bourgeoisie is less belligerent than indifferent to the fate of the masses – less cynical than self-centred on its own material concerns. In reality, it has quietly moved towards Mrs Thatcher's 'no society'. Little by little, the winners of the economic model, the distant heirs of an enlightened bourgeoisie, are abandoning the values that in the last century still held together a coherent society, a society where the dominant classes had not seceded and were still working for the common good; a society where class conflict provided a sense of structure and where elites were not systematically perceived as enemies but sometimes as fellow travellers. The Communist Party of yesterday is there to remind us that not only was this alliance possible, but also that the working classes have never denounced the 'elites' merely on principle.

It is the contemporary elites that the working classes criticize, certainly not elitism per se. In the service of the common good, the Gaullist–Communist elites, to whom we owe the major industrial and development advances of the post-war period, won the working-class vote. The same goes for cultural elites. We only need to compare the representation of the working classes in French cinema today and in that of yesterday to convince ourselves that it is indeed the elites who have turned their backs on ordinary people and not the other way around.[10]

The rejection of social otherness and indifference to ordinary people are certainly what best define today's ruling and upper classes. This rejection lies behind the shift in society towards a new world, where truly social interactions are shrinking like the piece of shagreen leather in Balzac's novel.[11] If we had to choose a single indicator of the record of the bourgeoisie, of its social footprint, it would be that of the exclusion of the working classes.

During the recent Covid crisis, physical distancing measures, otherwise known as 'social distancing', were put in place in order to distance individuals from each other. Aimed at stopping or slowing down the contagious virus, this policy reduced contacts by closing schools and workplaces and by restricting movement. The negative effects of these measures have been widely commented on: loneliness, depression, atomization, anomie, and a drastic drop in the human interactions that make up society. Today, having finally emerged from the health crisis, we are still in a society of distancing.

The territorial organization, the invisible walls, the monopolization of wealth, the eviction of the working classes from places of economic power and cultural representations, all demonstrate that tomorrow's world is already here – the world of 'social distancing', of distance from the Other. In many ways, the working classes are considered to be carriers of a virus: the virus of the questioning of the dominant model or, worse, the virus of hatred. An invisible sanitary cordon (cultural, political and geographical) has gradually been put in place.

This social state of distancing, where the upper classes and the working classes almost never cross paths, is – even more than the unemployment rate of the latter – the most important and the most telling indicator of the social imprint of the bourgeoisie.

This anti-world, which rejects social otherness, and in which ordinary people are told that they 'are nothing',[12] that they have no place, is the fruit of a Faustian pact signed in the 1980s, with its unconditional acceptance of market logic at the price of abandoning the common good and the principles of equality. If it has proved materially profitable, this pact has also stripped the upper strata of a form of transcendence, of values that were equally held by the traditional or progressive bourgeoisies, right and left. By submitting to the imperatives of the commodity and to them alone, the dominant and upper classes have abandoned everything that makes sense in a society (the common good, public service, secularism, the nation). The social impact is now clearly visible.

Part II
The fog

Rejecting the slightest reform of a model that nevertheless causes irreversible social damage, the upper strata continue on their way, taking care to eliminate the traces of their damage. In the manner of large polluting companies that mask their environmental footprint with green communication and the financing of ecological projects, they seek to make their responsibility disappear behind a false narrative. From the greenwashing of multinationals to the socialwashing of the dominant and upper classes, the objective is the same: to erase the footprints and evidence of the crime. This subtle enterprise does not involve any kind of ban or the creation of a 'Potemkin society',[1] but the spreading of an artificial fog that modifies the contours of the real world. A part of reality, the reality of ordinary people, becomes blurred. And, in this saturated and toxic, imperceptible air, the destruction of ordinary life continues.

Many are those artisans who play a part in the creation of this cloud of unreality, which simultaneously affects the media and the political, cultural, technocratic and academic worlds. In fact, anything that can confuse, complicate and reduce society to a mass of atoms, trend sheets and individuals, anything that can transform reality into smog, is welcome.

Political discourse, increasingly vague and meaningless, fits perfectly into this forest of clouds. No longer aiming to represent the ordinary majority but rather to protect and perpetuate the economic model, the ruling political class seems to have come together in a new party, the Fog Party. In France, for example, Macronism, that party of 'at the same time', of everything and its opposite, of the right *and* the left, of liberalism as well as statism, of 'whatever the cost', of contradictory injunctions (they reached a peak in the Covid crisis), of the denunciation but also of the fabrication of fake news, of tomorrow's world and the end of the world, is its embodiment.

The activists of the Fog Party are numerous, in France and all over the world. Unlike in past centuries, the ruling elites rely less on ideologies than on this cotton wool of unreality to impose their model. Global governance no longer involves politics and ideas, but rather this fog. The goal is no longer to convince, but to impose a spectacle that will allow us to remain firm as to essentials: the preservation of the economic model, of the laissez-faire market. The reign of falsehood, of masks, sometimes of lies, of 'washing' (greenwashing, social washing, so-called diversity) leads us to fall into the great narrative of a parallel world with its codes and representations. A world where ordinary society, the one that is being ransacked in social and cultural terms, has disappeared, swallowed up in the fog.

4
Cinema

All nations, all peoples have been built on stories and myths. People also talk of the national narrative and even of the national novel. All countries have thus forged their identity from historical episodes, legends, prestigious ancestors, by obscuring a greater or lesser part of reality. The American national novel, from the Quakers and the Pilgrim Fathers to the 'American way of life' promoted by Hollywood, focuses on a single story, that of the WASP. By obscuring the indigenous presence, this story allows the United States to be presented as a fundamentally moral power. In France, it was primary school that was partly responsible, at the end of the nineteenth century, for constructing the national narrative and unifying regions with different languages and identities (Brittany, Occitania, the Basque Country, etc.), in particular by highlighting the epic of heroes (from Vercingetorix to Napoleon), who were supposed to embody a glorious history and to exalt patriotism. In the Netherlands, the national narrative was partly constructed on the economic epic of city merchants.

For his part, the Israeli historian Shlomo Sand[1] shows how the creation of Israel was based on the mythical story of a Jewish population united by the same origin, the same land. His work highlights the impasse of ethnocentrism in the construction of the national novel, and indirectly echoes the thoughts of the French historian and philosopher Marcel Gauchet for whom 'there are no origins, there are antecedents [. . .] and no historian is, for example, stupid enough to give a date of birth for the first Frenchman'.[2] Gauchet also notes that the notion of a 'national novel' is unfortunate, since, as he continues, 'all history takes the form of a story, but this story has the particularity of seeking to be true'.

This is an essential point: the national novel is not just a fable that we tell ourselves to enhance our self-esteem and/or refuse to see reality. It must be based on facts and relationships with other countries. It is therefore embodied in a human story. In France, for about fifteen years, national identities and stories have been constantly debated. The last time, in 2016, it was the need to rewrite the history curriculum that was raised. This debate got bogged down in just a few days. Gauchet attributed this failure to the debaters' desire to draw a contrast between an 'ethnocentrism of the past' and an 'ethnocentrism of the present',[3] by moving from the national novel to the fable of multiculturalism. If these intellectual struggles over the themes of the national identity and the national narrative regularly lead to a dead end and rekindle democratic malaise, it is in particular because they obscure a blind spot: the sidelining of the people who carry, embody and bring to life our values and our ways of life, namely the working classes.

From narrative to cinema

The contemporary national narrative of Western countries is less disturbed by the diversity of origins of the populations than by the invisibility of their majority blocs. 'With globalization', notes Gauchet, 'the axis of all societies has shifted from history to geography. We now define ourselves by the place we occupy in the world, initially forgetting that this place is a function of the past'[4] – a past that is fading with the increasing invisibility of the ordinary majority, of its internal exodus from the centre to the peripheries.

This internal exile, geographical but also mental, has taken the form of a massive political and cultural disaffiliation. The idea that 'this system is no longer for us' has gradually spread to all working-class circles.

This anthropological shift has freed the ruling classes, who no longer have to think about those who embody the long term. Indeed, what sets the contemporary narrative apart is not only that it no longer promotes a glorious history, but constructs a storyline freed from the constraints of ordinary life.

Since this narrative no longer needs true facts, the ruling class can then reshape reality, even free itself from it, and give free rein to a free-floating narrative. From the national novel to the metaverse, via Emmanuel Macron's injunction to 'think spring', the upper strata impose a disembodied narrative in which they can impose their representations, look at themselves and, on occasion, rewrite History. Nothing is ever completely false, people work with half-truths, they give the impression of dealing with reality, they even launched a few years ago the great 'anti-fake news' operation, which allows them to delicately impose the cool by-product of the Ministry of Truth. The objective is not to radically impose an ideology, but first and foremost to give the impression of reality. This subtle, vague narrative produces a daily fog through which reality becomes imperceptible. This narrative, guided at bottom by market logic, is a spectacle; not a live spectacle, but a moral spectacle, an industrial, advertising-driven form of entertainment – in short, it is cinema.

Their cinema

The diffusion of the dominant ideology by the media as well as the critique of that ideology are nothing new. While everyone agrees on the obviousness of the propaganda of totalitarian regimes, the narrative of democratic regimes is more difficult to critique.

In 1974, in his *Scritti corsari* (*Corsair Writings*), Pier Paolo Pasolini attacked the power of the medium that was then becoming dominant: television. Nowadays, it is enough to replace the word 'television' with 'social networks' or 'news channels' to glimpse the relevance of the analysis.

> Something terrible emanates from television. Something worse than the terror that must have been roused, in bygone centuries, by the mere idea of the Inquisition's special tribunals. There is indeed, in the depths of this same 'television', something similar to the spirit of the Inquisition: a clear, radical, sharp division between those who can be accepted and those who cannot: only the imbecile, the hypocrite, capable of saying phrases and words that are mere empty sound, can be accepted [. . .]. And it is here that television accomplishes the neo-capitalist discrimination between the good and the bad [. . .]. The televised ideological bombardment is not explicit: it consists entirely in things, and is entirely indirect. But never has a 'model of life' seen its propaganda spread with as much efficiency as through television. [. . .]. It is precisely because it is purely pragmatic that televised propaganda represents the moment of indifferentism of the new hedonistic ideology of consumption [. . .]. It's a powerful means of ideological diffusion, and precisely of the consecrated ideology of the dominant class. From the moment when someone listens to us on their television set, they have a relationship of inferior to superior towards us that is a terribly anti-democratic relationship [. . .] It is through the spirit of television that the spirit of the new power is concretely mani-

fested. There is no doubt that television is more authoritarian and repressive than any means of information in the world has ever been.[5]

Pasolini did not imagine, then, the place that the media industry would occupy a few decades later. Today, those in a position to speak have an almost infinite range of media, from streaming platforms to social networks, permanently feeding a narrative that aims to justify the economic model of the market, and its corollary, the consumer society. This media firepower is also a weapon of mass destruction, particularly of working-class culture. Pasolini again:

> No fascist centralism has managed to do what the centralism of consumer society has done. Fascism proposed a model, reactionary and monumental, but which remained a dead letter. The different particular cultures (peasant, sub-proletarian, working class) continued imperturbably to identify with their models, because repression was limited to obtaining their adherence in words. Today, on the contrary, adherence to the models imposed by the centre is total and unconditional. True cultural models are denied. The abjuration is accomplished. We can therefore affirm that the 'tolerance' of the hedonistic ideology desired by the new power is the worst repression in all of human history. But how could such repression have been exercised? Through two revolutions, which took place within the bourgeois organization: the revolution of infrastructures, and the revolution of the information system. [. . .] Through television, the centre has assimilated the entire country, which was historically very differentiated and very rich in original cultures. A great work of perfectly authentic and real normalization has begun and [. . .] it has imposed its models: models promoted by the new industrial class, which is no longer content with a 'consumer' but which also claims that other ideologies than that of consumption are unacceptable. [. . .]

> The Italians have enthusiastically accepted this new model imposed on them by television [. . .]. Let us take an example: the sub-proletarians, until recently, respected culture and were not ashamed of their own ignorance; on the contrary, they were proud of their working-class model of illiterates who nevertheless apprehended the mystery of reality. It was with a certain brazen contempt that they looked at the 'rich kids', the petty bourgeois, from whom they differentiated themselves, even when they were forced to serve them. Today, on the contrary, they are beginning to be ashamed of their ignorance: they have abjured their cultural model [. . .].[6]

If Pasolini perfectly described the process of acculturation of the working classes, he did not live to witness an even more insidious and radical enterprise, that of their erasure from history. Freed from the people, from their demands, and from their culture, the ruling class was able to set about writing a new world. In a 'depopulated', virgin landscape, the fields of possibility are unlimited: the invention of a new society and that of a new people can be envisaged.

The class that has the monopoly on speech can now start the show; the great cinema of unreality can begin.

All this already seems (very) distant, but a little detour through the 'Covid crisis' provides some perfect illustrations of the construction and functioning of this storytelling.

Let's go back to March 2020. The French population is under lockdown. However, there are some stories that will get more of a hearing than others. From the first days, the media are scrabbling over the 'lockdown diaries' of Leïla Slimani[7] and Marie Darrieussecq,[8] giving the floor to Brigitte Macron who finds the period a 'challenge',[9] and questioning intellectuals and experts on this time of suspended animation and on the meaning of life. Field surveys flesh out the picture a little by interviewing senior executives who telework from their secondary residences in Brittany or Var. Concealing the fact that the majority of the population is absolutely not concerned by this new way of organizing work,[10] the media tell us about the emergence of a new world. There is a need to rethink everything, psycho-philosophical reflections on what will come next become common, and the framework of what will come next will, unsurprisingly, be the living spaces of the upper classes.

As in most French films set in the 'provinces', the Parisian's secondary residence is the main setting for the action, while ordinary society is kept in the background, and merely glimpsed in passing (however, during the pandemic, it had the dubious privilege of being the 'first in line').

For decades, the narrative of the world of influencers has been that of the bourgeoisie. The entire 'expert' narrative, and the media and cultural narratives, are worked on and polished by the same circles, creating a multifaceted narrative that contributes to imposing a representation compatible with the dominant model. When think tanks (left and right), all funded by the CAC 40 stock market index (from Terra Nova to the Institut Montaigne and the Fondation Jean-Jaurès)[11] work, under a scientific veneer, to 'make the working-class populist', the audiovisual industry produces films in which the working classes are, at best, embodied by stereotypically miserable characters, at worst mocked or stigmatized. But, in each of these stories, society will be read through the distorting lenses of a bourgeoisie in thrall to the inegalitarian liberal model. All the cultural segments of a fragmented society are highlighted, except the traditional working classes. As Éric Neuhoff humorously sums it up,[12] today 'the typical pitch of French cinema is a one-legged Eritrean who arrives in Marseilles and sleeps with a middle-class woman'. Such films interest no one and are shown to empty cinemas, but each in its own way feeds a grand narrative in which the negative impact of the model of the dominant classes on ordinary life is hidden.

This bourgeois narrative is articulated on two levels: the spectacle produced by the entertainment industry (Hollywood, public audiovisual media) as well as the so-called 'scientific' analysis produced by the 'experts' ('think-tankers' from the media or academia).

Netflix, Gaumont, *Plus belle la vie*,[13] the *grandes écoles*, and Terra Nova all feed the same narrative and have the same objective: the creation of a new society, if possible deconstructed into sample groups and therefore compatible with the demands of the market. By creating this parallel world, big business and the bourgeoisie protect each other by feeding the media fog, its debates and its productions, all of which impose a fake world, blind to ordinary reality.

It is in this factory that all the marketing representations of the tribalized and fragmented society transmitted by the supporters of today's 'woke' world have gradually been imposed. These soldiers of cultural liberalism (the other side of economic liberalism),[14] most of them from the bourgeoisie, benefit from the benevolence of big business. From Adidas to Disney, from McDonald's to Facebook, from Google to Uber, from luxury goods company LVMH to Ikea, every multinational helps to produce this narrative, whose ultimate goal is less the deconstruction than the creation of a parallel reality where the social impact of the economic choices of the bourgeoisie is hidden. Influenced by this bourgeois, liberal and deconstructed aestheticism, the story of the world is now merging with the chronicle of the virtual.

The transclass, an Oscar-worthy role

As in the cinema, the objective is to maintain the illusion through a very precise staging and distribution of roles, particularly the role of the working classes – a minor role that will suggest reality, but without ever calling into question the model. The Victor Hugo figure of the *misérables* can now enter the scene. As unconscious players in the media fog, the *misé-*

rables, the poor and the marginalized who manage against all the odds to extract themselves from their environment, have become ubiquitous. Their social origin, their difficulties, and ultimately their success, make it possible to give credibility to the storytelling. This instrumentalization of the poor by the bourgeoisie is not new but, in a period when the working classes are being pushed out, it appears as a centrepiece of the show.

It was in a famous speech given in 1963 in Detroit that Malcolm X first mentioned the figure of the 'house Negro', the servant whom he contrasted with the 'field Negro', who worked on plantations.[15] This term was intended to criticize those who indirectly legitimized white domination, and was part of the very particular context of American racialism. But, while the expression is a radical one, it points to a universal process, that of the instrumentalization of the exploited, the weak, and the poor by the dominant. The figure of the poor man or woman who legitimizes the social order is an old story: it has been exploited by all powers, by all bourgeoisies, whatever the era. Ours is no exception. Today, from the figure of the transclass[16] to that of the poor whiner holding out his hand, the miserabilist, submissive figure of the working classes is still relevant. The house pauper, who mourns his or her condition by legitimizing the very same model that impoverishes them, saturates our screens.

Not a day goes by without the broadcasting[17] of some poignant testimony from a 'kid', male or female, 'who didn't know the rules' but, despite all the obstacles, managed, like Jack London, to access bourgeois life. With tears in their eyes, the commentators do not have enough words to express their admiration for this writer, artist, cook, or business executive, who has just managed to work his or her way up from the bottom. Focusing on the representation of this individual from the working-class world (in the case of the older ones), from the suburbs or from peripheral France (with the younger ones), proves that, with a little courage, everything is possible. What is striking is the timing of this drama. Indeed, it's just as the social elevator is breaking down, the meritocratic model is imploding, and the working classes are being sacrificed that we see more and more of these extraordinary examples from ordinary society. These puppets, who allow the winners and pillars of a destructive model to ease their bad consciousness a little (when it exists), are everywhere. The message is very clear: society is harsh and inegalitarian, but it is not closed, and everything is possible with a little will-power ('where there's a will, there's a way').

As a media circus phenomenon, the figure of the transclass fits perfectly into this Americanized audiovisual story of representations of the upper strata. The showcasing of the self-made man is still an old ploy of the British and American worlds.

This figure of the class defector is a creation of the bourgeoisie for the bourgeoisie; it feeds a market (press and publishing) whose readers still come overwhelmingly from the upper classes, active or retired (the winning sociological combo of Macronism). This bourgeoisie, which has seceded from the lower strata, and systematically demonizes working-class protest when it is expressed in the streets or at the ballot box, is mesmerized by the journey of these 'kids who have succeeded'. (Note the constant reference to childhood, suggesting the infantilization of these puppets.)

In this role playing, the elevation of the ordinary individual is dependent on adherence to the codes of the bourgeoisie, its culture and its values: the red carpet is unrolled for the class defector who, while overplaying his attachment to the 'lower class', will condemn the intolerance, homophobia, racism, and stupidity of his background, obviously affected by anomie, and prone to social and cultural decay. This picture will be opportunely completed with small 'sensitive', 'psychological' or dramatic touches that will evoke suffering, pain, and always humiliation: Dad toiled for a pittance, Mum did the housework, the kid sister takes drugs and the little brother's in jail. Between mawkish pity and remakes of *Ugly, Dirty and Bad*,[18] little consideration will be given to what George Orwell called 'common decency' and even less to the idea that being born into a working-class environment can also be a blessing, that you can lead a life in it and even flourish. Before explaining to young people from working-class backgrounds that 'if you haven't joined the middle class by the age of fifty, you're a failure', wouldn't it be useful, on the contrary, to promote the strength and richness of working-class culture? Before highlighting the marginal figure of the self-made man, couldn't we instead explain to 'kids' that you can be born, live and die in a working-class environment and still succeed in life?

Moreover, one might wonder what is the point of this 'spewing up of private life',[19] if not to endorse the story of a society that has abandoned the common good and, ultimately, to exalt a model based on a bourgeois individualism perfectly adapted to the needs of the market? The extraordinary individual from the ordinary world is first and foremost a character quick to play the social game to which he or she is assigned, which often reveals less their courage than their conformism. And, after all, if it is so difficult for these modern heroes to frequent the bourgeoisie, why do they put themselves through this hell?

Jack London is often referred to as a kind of incarnation of the class defector, of the individual journey that defies the logic of social reproduction. The bourgeoisie was also infatuated with his autobiographical novel, *Martin Eden*, in which they believed they could perceive a man's desire to join the upper class – the great adventure of a self-made man, and thus, implicitly, the illustration of its own open-mindedness. This is a complete misinterpretation. The power of this novel actually lies in its radical critique of an individualistic bourgeoisie guided by money. Jack London would express this rejection of the bourgeoisie and its values, in particular in *What Life Means to Me*,[20] a brief autobiography in which he recounts how and why he experienced middle-class life at first hand, describing what he saw and the dark conclusions he drew from it.

Bitterly, he compares the mediocrity of the upper strata to the superiority of the values of working-class society, of the 'wild world'. A repentant transclass figure, the American novelist actually caused the narrative and ideology of the upper classes to implode.

If the figure of the class defector endorses and fuels the narrative of the dominant classes, that of the one who repents makes it completely implode. These repentant class defectors exist, but they are rare; as rare as flying fish. J. D. Vance is a flying fish. Published in 2016, in the middle of Donald Trump's campaign, his autobiography *Hillbilly Elegy* offered American elites a rational and ultimately reassuring explanation for Trump's victory.[21] For the media, which had not perceived the social and cultural weakening of the white working class of peripheral America (located between the two seaboards and outside the major cities), this text is a revelation. Sold in millions of copies, celebrated by the progressive intelligentsia, adapted into a Netflix film that won an Oscar,[22] it tells the story of the end of a world, that of the 'hillbillies', the impoverished little white folk from Appalachia hit by deindustrialization, ravaged by unemployment and decimated by the abuse of opiate drugs. It was precisely this 'endgame', this destruction – poignant, yes, but definitive – of useless social categories that reassured the elites. The 'deplorables' have indeed lost the game, their culture has failed to adapt, and this book is their swan song.

Indeed, the end of the working class fits perfectly into the story of the American dominant and media class. The character of J. D. Vance too. The author ticks all the boxes of the self-made man. A perfect defector, he broke away from his background, climbed the corporate ladder and, after a stint at Harvard, even made his fortune in Silicon Valley. This exemplary career path illustrates the relevance of the meritocratic – but also economic – model. Vance even supported Hillary Clinton and opposed Donald Trump, whom he compared to heroin: 'There is no self-reflection in the midst of a false euphoria. Trump is cultural heroin. He makes some feel better for a bit. But he cannot fix what ails them, and one day they'll realize it', he wrote in 2016 in *The Atlantic*.[23] By espousing the dominant values of the progressive bourgeoisie and rejecting his culture of origin, he was quite logically anointed and hailed by the bourgeoisie.

But, six years later, the hero made a radical U-turn. He ran for the Senate as a Republican and even took up Donald Trump's themes (outsourcing, criticism of the media), accused Joe Biden of promoting illegal immigration and the trafficking of Fentanyl, a synthetic drug that was wreaking havoc. During his campaign, he explained his change of heart: he hadn't liked Donald Trump in 2016, like many Republicans, but he had been honest enough to admit his mistake.

The question here is not to examine the political machinations and electoral strategies of a candidate changing his views to suit an electorate, nor to know if Trump is right or wrong, but to analyse the reaction of the media and the intelligentsia, who yesterday praised J. D. Vance to the skies, only to pillory him today. What is interesting is this radical U-turn, which perfectly illustrates the function of these defectors. Rejecting the codes of the dominant class, its story no longer fitting into the narrative, the penitent transclass is no longer of interest. Beyond this predictable reaction, Vance's journey recalls that of Jack London. He played the game, he embodied the mythology of American success, he integrated into the elite, he adopted their values, and he finally abandoned them.

Like London a century ago, Vance sought to embrace all the moral and cultural codes of an environment that was not his own, in order to ultimately conclude that the values held by his original environment were superior to those of the middle class. Vance's disappointment is certainly less profound and perhaps less sincere than London's, but it perfectly illustrates the limits of the role that the transclass must play: that of an individual who not only endorses the dominant model and narrative, but who must above all present his culture of origin as weak and outdated. These are limits that tolerate no improvisation, no cultural deviation.

The realm of whiners

It is within this rigid and limited cultural framework that the authorized expression of the working classes is played out today. The staging of the lower-class characters who succeed in life illustrates what is expected of them. These moving and harmless people are eternal victims, and play only a minor role.

When it is mentioned by the mainstream media, the social question is never treated as a consequence of the choices of the ruling elites, but as an immersion in Victor Hugo's world, the world of Jean Valjean and Cosette.

This universe allows us to reduce the social question to an outburst of emotion or, to be clearer, to whining. Today, the treatment of social issues by the media systematically passes through this category of 'emotion'. Remember how the Yellow Vests insurrection, after having been initially demonized, gradually led to a sentimental pity for the people who composed it. Desperate rural mayors, destitute OAPs, single Mother Courages, and poor employees were allowed to speak, not about the model crushing them, the exploding inequalities, the unbearable social injustice, but exclusively about their misery – if possible with tears in their eyes.

These 'TV moments' generally ended with a sequence redolent of 'generosity' (with, as a highlight, the presidential showpiece of the 'great debate'): the government would promise, hand on heart, to resolve these scandalous personal situations by signing cheques. Whining, in other words, and at the same time a reaffirmation of the social order, with the poor begging for subsidies and welfare from those in power.

None of this is new. Since the liberal shift of the 1980s, the tearful representation of the working classes seems to sum up the social question all by itself.

Because whining is not the prerogative of peripheral France, it is also at the heart of the authorized expression of the suburbs. In a few years, media sentimentality has performed the feat of reducing these great historical bastions of the workers' struggles of the Communist Party to a nice little office of tears.

In a perfectly rehearsed scenario, most often after a few days of riots, emotional journalists hold out their microphones to those willing to explain that 'we've got nothing', 'neither present nor future'. During the Covid crisis, the prefect of Seine-Saint-Denis went even further in escalating this miserabilism by evoking the risk of 'food riots'. It must be said that this *département*, Saint-Denis, has become a sort of benchmark for the tearful representation of the working classes in France. Too bad for the reality.

Too bad, for example, that the economic and geographical situation of this *département* has completely changed. Due to the metropolitanization and geographical extension of the urban area, Seine-Saint-Denis is no longer on the sidelines of the economic system of the Paris region but at its very centre, at the heart of the most active job market in the country, one of the richest big cities in the world. This *département* is inserted into the cogs of the economy and is home to the biggest head offices – even better, it has been 'producing' the middle class for decades. This upwardly mobile social category is obviously not visible, since it moves out of neighbourhoods plagued by violence and trafficking as quickly as possible, but it proves that living in the heart of a dynamic job market automatically offers opportunities. In reality, Seine-Saint-Denis perfectly meets neo-liberal requirements, providing the metropolitan job market with a cheap and constantly renewed workforce. Far from the media image, it appears as the vanguard of the globalized capitalist model, in which there is a high degree of mobility.

Indeed, like all the neighbourhoods of those big cities labelled 'sensitive' (unlike neighbourhoods in medium or small cities whose poverty rates are much higher), this *département* is an 'airlock' that many people leave (households integrated into the job market) and that many people come into (legal and illegal international immigrants).

This 'airlock function', where those people in situations that are 'a little less precarious' are permanently replaced by 'even more precarious' households, explains its social portrait: the 'stock' of poor and unemployed people is constantly being renewed. This is not an anomaly: it responds to the demands of the market, including the demands of the informal economy (in Seine-Saint-Denis, the turnover of drug trafficking is estimated at one billion euros).[24] This *département*, the spearhead of globalized capitalism and its societal model (the communitarian model), with an administration that is subcontracted by 'anti-capitalist' elected officials (left or far left), is also the quintessence of a model where money, the market – including the black market – is king. It also illustrates the role that the ruling elites want the working classes to play: that of atomized or, even better, communitarian actors, who will only ever express themselves in the public and political space to whine and demand new rights – on condition that they never question the dominant order.

In reality, from the Yellow Vests to the rioters in the cities, from rural mayors to suburban elected officials, there is only one thing asked of the working classes: to whine in front of the cameras without ever questioning the model that sacrifices them socially.

They are kindly invited to abandon a precious commodity: their dignity. This cultural hara-kiri of individuals who tell everyone that they have *nothing*, that they are *nothing*,[25] completes the deconstruction of the working-class world.

If there is no shame in being poor, there is no pride in being poor either. What mechanism is it that leads individuals to this exhibitionism, if not the pressure of the television show scripted by the upper classes?

In real life, ordinary people actually seek to preserve their dignity, and rarely exploit their difficulties. It is to the oh-so-compassionate register of the bourgeoisie that this indecent staging of poverty belongs. The dominant class – yesterday Catholic, today progressive or left-wing – establishes its moral superiority and legitimizes its domination by substituting this weak and tearful figure of the poor for the solid working-class bloc. The ridiculous insistence with which experts, journalists, politicians, producers and film directors award Seine-Saint-Denis the glorious medal of 'the poorest *département* in France' is typical of this petty-bourgeois paternalism. Ultimately, this rhetoric allows the inhabitants of these territories to be reduced to simple consumers of goods and social benefits, by ignoring the ordinary workers who live in these neighbourhoods – ordinary people who do not recognize themselves in these tearful representations, and even less in that of the 'young rebel' that the media love to highlight. Fantasized by the progressive bourgeoisie, this figure horrifies the ordinary immigrant worker, who is exasperated by the delinquents who poison his life and those of his children.

But, for opinion leaders, the reality of peripheral France, where the poorest neighbourhoods of the country are concentrated and where precariousness has become embedded as th labour market deteriorates, has lost its importance. Who cares, for example, about the situation of social housing districts in Saint-Dizier? Certainly not the media experts and even less the show-biz world, whose members would not know where to find this city on a map. For their information, Saint-Dizier is a town of 25,000 inhabitants, located in the *département* of Haute-Marne, in the Grand Est region, halfway between Paris and Strasbourg. Do they also know that the overseas *départements* are the poorest in France?²⁶ That poor people also live in Aude, Pas-de-Calais or Cantal? They would most certainly be surprised to learn that, in poor rural areas, social benefits are underused.²⁷

Pity and social exhibitionism fit together impeccably in a society where victimization has become the norm, almost *the* condition of existence. Stripped of their dignity, individuals no longer define themselves by what they are but by being represented as victims, following the dictates of the market. In this context, individuals no longer accept the reality principle and are no longer responsible for their actions or their destiny; they define themselves as the product of the social or cultural aggressions they suffer. In this infinite line-up of paranoid victims, the wretched origin of individuals also becomes social and media capital. 'Dad's a worker', or 'unemployed', 'Mum's a cleaner' or 'a nanny' – and that means I'm entitled to recognition, compassion and perhaps even reparations. A tearful annuity for life, and for several generations perhaps? 'My great-grandmother didn't eat her fill', 'my grandfather worked eight-hour shifts' – and I'm surely entitled to something, to my minute of glory on a news channel?

Humiliating and abject in many ways, this staging allows the 'social' to be scripted without worrying about the substance. Like the greenwashing of the most polluting multinationals, this 'social washing' allows social demands to be replaced by an ultimately inexpensive victimization.

This instrumentalization is reminiscent of the famous 'everyday heroes' that the media urged us to applaud during the Covid crisis. These caregivers, cashiers, delivery people, rubbish collectors and other ordinary people even had their moment of glory thanks to the way they were given priority as key workers. The compassionate treatment of their working conditions obscured the social issue, and this media appearance has not led to any salary increase, and even less to any questioning of the health or economic model.

Between miserabilism and whining, the fog of compassion completes the picture of a weak and whiny ordinary majority. But this glorious portrait of the working classes is incomplete, and still lacks one essential element: suggesting that this majority does not even exist.

5
'There is no majority'

In May 2019, Mark Zuckerberg arrived at the Élysée Palace. The founder of Facebook was received like a head of state by President Emmanuel Macron, whose obsequiousness left no doubt about who was the boss and who was the employee. This red carpet rolled out for the king of the American algorithm illustrates the growing importance of digital technology in political management. Modelling, the reduction of society to two binary computer values (the '0' and the '1'), acts like an acid on human reality.

The language that renders people invisible

No field is spared. For example, geography, so-called 'human geography', that which analyses the interactions between human beings and their environment or, as Pierre George wrote, 'the reciprocal relationships between population groups and their works',[1] undergoes the same 'dehumanization' by becoming a tool for analysing 'territories'. Technostructure experts now speak of 'territorial engineering'. The human dimension has given way to statistics, trend charts and other anamorphic maps – a dehumanized framework in which the geographical works of a Vidal de La Blache, an Élisée Reclus or an Edmond Bernus no longer have their place.[2] What link could there be between this literature and contemporary practice, which is nowadays limited to modelling territories?

This encrypted, technocratic language overcomplicates every subject, even the simplest, by making it inaccessible: work, housing, security, relationships with elected officials, the way of life in one's neighbourhood or municipality. Yesterday, all these themes of daily life were fully grasped by the ordinary majority, and people did not need external lighting to understand their reality. Today, the most basic questions are no longer dealt with by elected officials or residents but delegated to technicians, expert firms, specialists who turn what was clear yesterday into something incomprehensible. By invading all these areas of ordinary life, technocratic verbiage inevitably deprives individuals of speech, but it has the same effect on local elected officials. This semantic dispossession has reached a pinnacle in the economic field, and it has also reached a point of no return in the geographical field. By reducing human lives to the simple word 'territory', the technocratic and academic fog can evoke the 'social' sphere in its own way, putting on white gloves, for example, to speak of a 'working-class neighbourhood'. Sanitized, dehumanized, and technocratized, the whole 'working-class' world becomes the 'working-class neighbourhood'. It is rather piquant to hear elected officials present themselves as the representatives of these 'working-class neighbourhoods', borrowing the typical language of bourgeois technocracy. Let us note in this regard that the inhabitants of these 'neighbourhoods' are completely impervious and indifferent to this techno-political discourse: proof of this is their level of abstention at the polls. In the 2022 legislative elections, the NUPES,[3] which, despite its acronym, attracted fewer 'working-class' people than executives, intermediate professions and graduates,[4] achieved the grand slam in the 'working-class neighbourhoods' of Seine-Saint-Denis but to the general indifference of its inhabitants. In some constituencies of the *département*, abstention sometimes exceeded 75 per cent; a few lucky deputies were elected with less than ten per cent of registered voters,[5] which did not prevent them from flaunting the label 'working-class neighbourhoods'.

This strategy, which aims to reduce ordinary life to a 'territory', is not specific to the suburbs; the Yellow Vests soon became associated with a 'France of roundabouts'. The demonstrators who shouted 'We exist!' were thus reduced to a single setting, that of an ugly France, of the 'peri-urban', which is still a meaningless term (there are different types of 'peri-urban': the peri-urban area of Yvelines has nothing to do with that of Oyonnax). Seen from the vantage point of the middle classes, the revolt of the working classes was an opportunity to debate urban aesthetics, the ugliness of the areas where these 'deplorables' lived. This shift towards the 'territory' was accompanied by the highly effective, indeed indestructible argument based on the authority of complexity. A movement of the working classes? But it's much more complicated than that, my dear! What was so complicated? Nobody knows. But that wasn't the important thing, it was above all a question of regaining control, of re-legitimizing the knowledgeable and the powerful who hadn't seen any of what was coming.

No representation is neutral. By hiding behind the false objectivity of the scientist, the human science experts, political scientists, sociologists, pollsters and economists convey a vision: that of power. It is also in this war of representations that we must include the attacks on the concept of 'peripheral France'. This concept, which finally gave us a view of the reality of contemporary class struggle and the negative effects of the neoliberal model, was logically perceived as a danger by liberals and the so-called progressive left (which is in reality just as liberal).

Based not on 'territories' but on the spatial distribution of the working classes, this concept, which aims to embody and make visible a majority working-class France and to describe the consequences of the economic model on ordinary society, contradicts the representation in which this same majority has disappeared.

By announcing the end of politics more than forty years ago with her notorious slogan 'There is no alternative', then predicting the end of the common good with her no less notorious 'There is no such thing [as society]', British Prime Minister Margaret Thatcher foresaw the logical next step that would finally free the market from all constraints: the disappearance of ordinary people, the 'There is no majority' – the last step in the long way of the cross that leads to the assertion, now common among the ruling classes that 'the people do not exist'.

The parent company is Netflix

Since the ordinary majority no longer exists, anything that promotes the dissemination of a 'spreadsheet' representation of society is encouraged. It is mostly the entertainment industry that relies on this society, sliced up like a sausage. In this marketed archipelago (of tribes, minorities) where nothing makes sense, the working-class continent and the common good have disappeared.

But, to be sustainable, this delicate task, which endorses the inegalitarian model, needs to be accompanied by effective storytelling to explain the non-existence of a majority bloc – a moral and intellectual justification, in short. Wokeism, built on the defence of minorities, fulfils this function perfectly. The latest avatar of the war of representations, in the West it currently benefits from a promotion drive worthy of an American blockbuster.

Whether promoted or resisted, this wokeism is everywhere. Faithful to advertising techniques, its promoters know that the important thing is to *talk* about it, for good or bad, it doesn't matter; just to talk about it, and to saturate the media with themes that divide society into slices, into items in a spreadsheet. They launch divisive debates and concepts on a daily basis, since the important thing is not to convince anyone but to impose the idea of a new society, a new people, without ties or history. Presented as quite new, this representation is rarely analysed as part of a long-term project that tends to incorporate the societal model into its economic envelope, with the individual-consumer in place of the citizen.

The strength of this commercial representation lies in the way it can deck itself out in the finery of a philosophical thinking.

The intellectual genealogy of deconstruction naturally brings us back to the post-modernist philosophers of French Theory (Derrida, Beauvoir, Deleuze, Foucault) and gender studies. To justify this society of segments and minorities, it even occasionally places itself under the authority of Tocqueville and his 'tyranny of the majority' to justify its exclusion. This alleged tyranny, in passing, makes the working classes bear the responsibility for the totalitarianisms of the twentieth century (it is well known that national socialism, fascism and communism germinated in the sick brains of ordinary people . . .).

While these references dress up deconstruction in an intellectual garb, they obscure a much more powerful steamroller: the market. Without Nike, wokeness does not exist. In fact, it does not exist in society (ordinary people remain indifferent to this narrative).

Note, too, that this ideology, or rather this sales technique, only exists in the West. When it can impact their sales, as is the case in China or in Muslim countries, the militant multinationals of the woke world are perfectly able to be discreet on the subject. Without qualms, they can abandon their woke codes to promote 'Islamically correct' marketing (selling a sports hijab, like Nike), to avoid offending Xi Jinping (having the British Tilda Swinton play a Tibetan character from *Doctor Strange*, like Marvel Studios) or to whitewash a blockbuster (hiding the black actor John Boyega on the poster for *Star Wars: The Force Awakens*, like the Walt Disney Company).[6] Described as a new global totalitarianism, wokeism is in fact merely a symptom of the extension of the limits of the market in the West and the exclusion of the ordinary majority.

It is a deconstructive enterprise that is enthusiastically supported by the political world.

Always sailing along in the wake of the multinationals, politicians have not resisted the temptation of electoral marketing. Following the advice of think tanks financed by the CAC 40 stock market index, their electoral strategies have gradually aligned themselves with commercial sales methods. Political parties will no longer address a majority, but rather spreadsheets.

Today, the parent company of the political narrative in the West is Netflix. The so-called progressive candidates, who are supposed to win elections to ensure the sustainability of the model, host a programme and sell performances designed and produced in Los Angeles. In this regard, it is amusing to note that after his training internship at the White House, Barack Obama reached the next level and was given a position as a Netflix producer. Emmanuel Macron, who is merely the French President, has not yet reached this level but is preparing for it. In 2022, the Netflix candidate launched his campaign with a magnificent teaser that deployed all the trademark signs of the famous entertainment platform.

Last, but not least, Netflix was not content with its protégé Macron, long since committed to the cause, but also launched Jean-Luc Mélenchon. For, contrary to appearances, Mélenchonism fits perfectly with the storytelling of the entertainment industry, the trend chart, the intersection, the disappearance of the ordinary majority and especially the future world. This so-called 'Terranovesque'[7] commercial strategy is quite simple. It involves targeting social or cultural groups to reach a relatively low minimum qualification threshold for the second round of the election (around 20%), then, if possible, finding yourself facing the populist candidate, and winning. But the problem is that marketing is not a project; targeting minority sample groups will never be a project. This explains why, even if elected, this type of Netflix candidate is always doomed to illegitimacy and destined to be sociologically, culturally, and geographically restricted. For, while the representation of a society divided into samples allows the central question of the ordinary majority to remain hidden for a while, it is still very much there – the proverbial elephant in the room.

Metropolises, those temples of the market and neoliberalism, have naturally become the playground of such candidates – their electoral strongholds. Ultra-marketed representation adapts admirably to these spaces that have long since been liberated from the working classes. At the beginning of the 2020s, in these gentrified cities, the upper classes are overrepresented. The working-class presence is today limited to populations of immigrant origin, who are concentrated in the last provision of the non-gentrified housing stock, namely the blocks of social housing. This very atypical and inegalitarian sociological profile is characteristic of metropolises. In these spaces where social divisions more or less coincide with ethnic divisions, everyone has their place. Contrary to what one might imagine, the so-called progressive bourgeoisie has absolutely no intention of making room for the immigrant working classes, but of using them: the buildings in which the members of this bourgeoisie live, the schools in which they educate their offspring, and even the working-class circles in which they are active, are generally socially and ethnically homogeneous. Maintaining a lumpenproletariat in the metropolises meets the need to employ an underpaid workforce that will keep entire sectors of the economy running (construction, catering) and provide cheap staff that are essential to the bourgeois lifestyle: Diwata does the housework, Fatoumata looks after the children – but, as we were already asking a few years ago, 'who will take care of hers?',[8] and to this day, we get no answer. Then there's Mourad for Uber trips – the operation is delegated to an American multinational, so it's cheaper; and Koffi – a legal or illegal immigrant, but most often the latter – for home dinner deliveries. This makes for a highly inegalitarian sociological profile in metropolises. On the one hand, there are the dominant and wealthy upper classes: as real-estate prices rise, their wealth protects them for several generations. On the other hand, there are the precarious minorities. Netflix candidates are duly adjusting their electoral strategies. In 2022, Macron addressed the traditional bourgeoisie, retirees and, on the fringe, minorities, while Mélenchon turned to the progressive bourgeoisie and, on the fringe, minorities, particularly Muslims. Mélenchon thus succeeded in marrying together quite different categories: bobos and minorities, the societal left and the Muslim vote.[9]

Quite in line with the electoral showbiz sponsored by Hollywood, the community vote props up these candidates. If, in the first round, 69 per cent of Muslims chose 'Mélenchon the anti-capitalist', in the second, 85 per cent of them voted for the capitalist Macron.

Minorities, already armed with capital reserves, have become the electoral reserve army of liberal power. But for how long? This alliance is fragile. It is conditioned by the maintenance of high levels of migration that renew the exploitable workforce by increasing the electoral significance of these populations and by the adhesion of minorities to the narrative of the increasingly fascist tendencies of the ordinary majority. However, on these two points, the ruling powers must face a reality that destabilizes this electoral calculation: immigration is today contested by public opinion (including immigrants); as for 'ordinary fascism', it is losing its effectiveness.[10] Furthermore, the 'intersectional' alliance between Neuilly-sur-Seine, Boboland and La Courneuve remains contradictory.

The utopia of a new people

The politically opportunistic compounding of an eco-woke petty bourgeoisie and working-class social categories attached to traditional values cemented by religion makes no sense. It is not sustainable, but remains an objective for a political class at the end of its tether. This compounding, which, according to certain Western democrats could produce a new electorate, echoes their project to create a 'new people', or even a new civilization – a crazy objective that the subversive German poet Bertolt Brecht, author of the famous 'Since the people vote against the government, the people must be dissolved', could never have seriously imagined.[11]

Whether desired or feared, a new people, that is to say a bloc that would make sense to a majority of the population, and which through its values and way of life would be capable of projecting society into a reassuring future, has not emerged. This observation does not mean that a demographic revolution is not underway. For thirty years, the intensification of extra-European migratory flows has profoundly changed the population of the territories receiving these populations. This transformation has been all the more rapid and visible because it took place at a time when the elites were destroying the conditions for assimilation by denigrating the cultures and lifestyles of the working classes into which new arrivals have always blended. The rest is history. The segmented, so-called multicultural society, was imposed – and with it, the society of mistrust. As the historian Robert Putnam demonstrated in the last century, this type of society automatically leads to the abandonment of the common good and ultimately to the dismantling of the welfare state (a dismantling that remains an objective of the current ruling classes). In this model, where the Other does not become the self, it is separatism and segmentation that are the norm, not the birth of a new people.

For to dissolve one people and create a new one, it is not enough to displace new populations; it is necessary to attract and agglomerate people, arouse their support for a new way of life and new values, for an emerging group. The essential element is attraction.

But what conclusion can we draw from the evolution of the territories that have welcomed new migratory flows for decades? They are merely airlocks, reception areas: they do not attract. These spaces are only drop-off points for international immigration. Whatever their origin, the working classes who live there, whether native or immigrant, do everything they can to escape from this 'new world'.

As soon as they can, upwardly mobile households try to leave their neighbourhoods and schools (for example, by sending their children to Catholic schools).[12] Civil servants try to avoid them (the state even goes so far as to offer a loyalty bonus to civil and military public servants who agree to stay in Seine-Saint-Denis).[13] As for the progressive bourgeoisie who continue to sing their praises, its members do not seem all that keen to live in them. Unless I am mistaken, none of the so-called 'sensitive' neighbourhoods has seen these upper classes move into them. The many bobolands of the metropolises, although located just a few minutes from these places, have, strangely enough, not been deserted by people eager to move into the aforesaid neighbourhoods. The same is true of the schools: nothing doing – the children of the progressive bourgeoisie are conspicuous by their absence.

The multiplication of these enclaves is less the effect of attraction for an imported way of life than the result of the migration policy of the elites and the denigration of the majority culture.

These enclaves (more hillbilly than Islamist) are just one of the facets of the great segmentation inherent in the model endorsed by the elites for half a century. They represent just one of the segments of the Hollywoodian cultural market in which the Adidas burkini is fully at home. If the communitarian model fits snugly into the Americanization of French society, this does not make it a model for the population.

The lack of cultural attraction that 'neighbourhoods' and new arrivals exert on society as a whole shows that the creation of a people grown 'above ground' is not going to happen anytime soon, at least not in the suburbs.

Obsessed with the creation of a new people, the ruling class has forgotten one essential point: there are only 'old' peoples who will always seek to preserve what they are, and who aspire to blend into the majority way of life, when it is made attractive. Indeed, an 'old' people is attractive only if it is respected. The difficulty is that, for half a century, the political, media, cultural and academic class has spent its time deconstructing and denigrating the ordinary majority and its culture. All that was missing for the picture to be complete was the folklorization of that culture.

Coming out of one's reserve

Welcome to the France that dances to country music!

If this practice is widespread[14] in peripheral France (as are all the associations that keep local cultures alive, including traditional dances), its specific treatment by the media is far from innocent. In recent years, everyone, from BFM TV to *Le Monde*,[15] from RFI to *L'Express*, has waxed lyrical in ever more articles on the 'success of country dancing' in the 'working-class France of the villages'.

The Yellow Vests worried people, the Stetson reassures them. From the symbol of protest to the – derisory – symbol of a generalized acculturation, the dominant class proposes the representation of a ridiculous and therefore powerless working-class world. But this 'sympathetic' folklorization is more perverse. It reinforces the image that the Western ruling elites have of the working classes of the peripheries, those they call the 'little White folk', a pejorative expression forged by the American bourgeoisie ('White trash') that actually suggests an intrinsically racist and intellectually deficient population. However, by evoking a traditional American imaginary, country music immediately plunges us into that of the little Whites, the Rednecks. From folklorization to redneckization, the media system validates the idea that the working-class bloc is now confined to the edge of the world. It is powerless and doomed to die out in the great acculturated reservation of peripheral France. Redneckization makes this exclusion morally acceptable. As in any reservation, the natives benefit from a minimum of redistribution (the 'rednecks' have to consume, that's all that is asked of them) and even public services, but it is understood that they are living on borrowed time and condemned by the forward march of History.

In a playful tone, the reassuring representation of the French 'yokel' wearing a Stetson and imitating the other 'redneck', the one who lives on the other side of the Atlantic, is in itself enough to justify the relegation of the ordinary majority. The worst of it is that the sneers of the upper middle class insist on how this acculturation has become entrenched. Coming from a class that for half a century has embraced all the values of the American model and that daily drinks in the 'Instagram–Amazon–*New York Times*' culture, this position is not without its piquancy!

The 'deplorables' still have a bright future ahead of them.

What newcomers would want to be like them: ridiculous, acculturated, ageing, anomic, without a future, without values? Who in Sweden, Great Britain, France, Germany could want to adopt the lifestyle of a German redneck, a Swedish hillbilly, a British racist or a French yokel? Nobody.

In the upper strata of society, despite the attempt to create, to bring about a 'new people', there is little grasp of the fact that people do not assimilate by abstractly adopting the values of the host country, but by trying to resemble a respectable neighbour, one who is respectable because he or she is economically integrated – and above all culturally respected.

The ordinary majority, when viewed as a set of 'deplorables', is not attractive. Conversely, when it is recognized and respected, it is, automatically.

That is why the Yellow Vest movement attracted working classes of all origins, who participated in the protest, leaving aside their sexual, racial or religious identities. Caricatured as a movement of little Whites, this movement, arising in peripheral France, and particularly active in overseas France, seduced a minor but still significant fraction of French people of Maghrebi or African origin living in mainland France.

All over the world, the dignity and power of working-class, so-called populist protests, are leading a fraction of minorities to free themselves from the dominant discourse.

We saw this in Great Britain, where Brexit was very widely acclaimed in all working-class circles, as well as in the United States, where nearly forty per cent of Latinos and a proportion of African-Americans joined Republican voters, whom the media presented as 'white supremacists'.

Because they can hierarchize their priorities, and free themselves for a time from their origins to challenge the economic and social order and thus reject the trap set by the upper strata, ordinary people respond masterfully, thanks to their survival instinct, to their programmed disappearance.

So those in power will have to try something else.

6

Apocalypse now

The ruling elites now play on fear. Their storytelling, which was already based on whining emotionalism, now more readily occupies this terrain. From mass entertainment to mass anxiety, the objective remains the same: to extract oneself from reality and manufacture consent. The sense of an imminent threat lies at the heart of a play in two acts.

Act I. Enter the Prince of Darkness

The demonization of the working classes and their aspirations not only sterilizes their vote, but above all, thanks to this paralysing ray, decrees the social death of those who would seek, from near or far, to defend them. Political action has been replaced by a discourse of fear in which the Devil hides in every detail of the diagnosis of ordinary people: a hackneyed but effective technique that allows successive governments to stay in power. At the opposite end of the spectrum from Baudelaire, who wrote that 'the cleverest ruse of the Devil is to persuade you he does not exist!'[1] their greatest trick is to make us believe that he *does* exist. Today, demonization is the basis of the political argument of power, its ultimate protection. Any challenge to the economic-societal model involves summoning the Devil.

Demonization is essential to maintaining the narrative, and permits the moral condemnation of any request, any proposal, even the most legitimate. To mention the difficulties of the rural world is to be a Pétainist; to talk about protecting jobs, particularly industrial jobs, is to be a nationalist; to describe social fragility or poverty in peripheral France is to be a populist. Satan is absolutely everywhere, even on the plates we eat off. The recent Fabien Roussel 'sequence' is a fine example of this.

In early January 2022, on the set of the Sunday political show on public television, Francis Letellier interviewed Fabien Roussel, the Communist candidate for the presidency, on what he thought of the fact that Emmanuel Macron was named personality of the year by *La Revue du vin de France* (*The Review of French Wine*) in recognition of his commitment to French wine. Here is an excerpt:

> 'A good president is a president who defends wine?' asks Letellier.
>
> 'I said to myself when I saw that, well, it's right to defend wine. I myself like to drink a glass of wine . . .'
>
> 'He likes two glasses!'
>
> 'Good wine, good meat, good cheese – that's what I mean by French gastronomy. But to have access to this nice food and drink, these gastronomic treats, you have to be able to afford them. So the best way to defend good wine, good gastronomy, is to ensure the French can afford them. And I say that the good and the beautiful are things everyone must be able to afford.'
>
> 'The associations that fight against alcoholism say that we need to do more, for example put prominent warnings on bottles of wine, like on cigarette packets. Would you be in favour of that?'

'Yes, I think we should have prevention campaigns to combat alcoholism. But good wine, like good meat – it's better to drink less wine so long as it's good wine, eat less meat but good meat. Drink French wine, [consume] French meat. But above all, everyone should be able to afford it – it's expensive.'

'But always in moderation: thanks to the Évin law, it's written everywhere.'[2]

'So it's a question of wages and pension. That's how we defend our gastronomy', concluded Fabien Roussel.[3]

In short, the Communist candidate said: 'Good wine, good meat, good cheese, that's French gastronomy, and the best way to defend it is to ensure the French can afford it.' Immediately, he was subjected to a barrage of criticism from all sides.

First, he was accused of trivializing alcohol, and this attack was far from trivial: on the contrary it's an invariant of class contempt, already used against the PCF in the last century. For the record, there was that day in February 1981, in Montigny-lès-Cormeilles, when Georges Marchais supported the outgoing mayor, Robert Hue, at a meeting and took advantage of it to denounce his opponents, notably socialists, who never stopped insulting Communist working-class voters by accusing them of being 'narrow-minded, uneducated, racist, brutal' and . . . 'alcoholics'!

Forty years later, it was the same left-wing bourgeoisie who accused Fabien Roussel of promoting alcohol.

But not only that. Such scandalized and moralizing postures also concern the mistreatment of animals, with reference to the supposed brutality of the working classes, as well as a veiled request to the followers of 'sausage-and-pinard' aperitifs, a trademark of the extreme right, which is seen as proof of the intrinsic racism of workers. In case you hadn't understood the message, the ecologist candidate for the primary, Sandrine Rousseau, added that by speaking in this way, Fabien Roussel was 'exclud[ing] an aspect of gastronomy that is found in France' and dropped this very heavy hint: 'Couscous is the favourite dish of the French.'

This demonization by the liberal left was far from insignificant; it was aimed at the Communist candidate, who for several months during the campaign had adopted the traditional line of the PCF of defending the working classes, of giving primacy to the social question over the societal question, of defending industrial jobs and economic sovereignty. No one was fooled: Fabien Roussel was attacked on his political programme, not on his alleged speciesist or racist remarks.

In reality, if the Dalai Lama wanted to be elected tomorrow on a programme of defending the interests of the working classes, he would be immediately and similarly demonized. In a few days, the Buddhist monk would be presented as the candidate of intolerance, the promoter of a society that excludes the other, in short as a barely masked representative of the extreme right. What matters here is not the messenger but the message, especially if it is a message sent by the working classes.

But, accusing people of fascism is a technique that comes in many forms. The ¡No pasarán! of the bourgeoisie is never addressed to any but the same people, the least well-off, whose own diagnosis of the situation has to remain at the least delegitimized and at best inaudible.

Economic protectionism, on the contrary, equated with fascism by the upper strata, is accepted and acclaimed when it aims, for example, to protect the world of culture. The cinema and music industries made in France promote openness to the world, but have protected themselves for almost half a century from the global free trade market. Here, 'national preference' is called 'cultural exception', and, as if by magic, it becomes morally acceptable.

Nationalism, another taboo cuss word, can be positively assessed in certain cases – since the beginning of the Russian invasion of Ukraine, for example.

The mental health of the world's main leaders is also

commented on in different ways. The senility of a Joe Biden will always be more relativized than the madness of a Donald Trump or a Vladimir Putin. In the same way, cases of paedophilia are more stridently denounced when they take place in working-class circles[4] than when they concern the circles of the progressive elite (the omertà that surrounded the Olivier Duhamel[5] or Jeffrey Epstein cases for years).

As we can see, the system therefore defends neither morality, nor principles, nor ethics, nor justice, but uses them as weapons of protection. Denouncing the supposed racism, sexism or fascism of an individual or a group does not aim to force them to retreat, but mainly to administer the social death of the individual or group involved. This good old Stalinist technique is spreading everywhere (from the political world to that of business, including universities and the culture) in order simply to kill off the competition, to flaunt its own 'progressive' pedigree and to display its own moral superiority.

The cherry on the cake is that this allows the social order to be legitimized by demonizing protest. Indeed, since at least the ratification of the Maastricht Treaty,[6] in the minds (and trend charts) of successive powers, no opposition to the model can now be permitted ('There is no alternative').

Since these powers no longer have the nation as their framework or the common good as their objective, and can no longer play on the illusion of alterating left- and right-wing governments[7] to divide the working classes, their last defence will consist of excluding them not politically, but morally. And to ensure that the Devil no longer wears Prada, but blue overalls.

In this way, the ruling elites are shifting the debate from the political to the moral realm: voting 'no' in the referendum on the TCE,[8] supporting the Yellow Vests, encouraging any candidate labelled 'populist' would in their view be 'stupid', 'suicidal', and above all 'immoral'.

For the working classes, the democratic impasse is less due

to the absence of an available political programme than to the moral condemnation of this programme.

Whatever the political label (Jean-Pierre Chevènement, Fabien Roussel, Marine Le Pen, etc.), candidates who defend a programme defending the ordinary majority are systematically demonized, and their voters are seen as guilty of an immorality that is difficult to maintain on a daily basis. This is why, even if, on most political and economic issues, a majority of the population agrees with 'populist' proposals (sovereignty, protectionism, reindustrialization, the regulation of migratory flows),[9] a fraction, particularly of older voters, will never cross this 'moral' line.

However, this fraction tends, from election to election, to decrease, and an appeal to the Devil no longer seems so effective.

On the occasion of the second round of the 2022 presidential election, thirteen million voters slipped a Marine Le Pen ballot into the ballot box, thirteen million abstained and two million preferred a blank vote.[10] In total, more than 28 million French people therefore 'voted for the wrong person'. Fifty-eight per cent of the electorate freed themselves from morality by not voting against the Devil. Two years earlier, in the United States, 74 million Americans (11 million more than in 2016) also chose to remove themselves from humanity to cast their vote for the blond-haired Beelzebub. (By abstaining, 80 million chose not to vote against him.)[11] In 2016, in Great Britain, the majority of British voters voted for 'withdrawal, hatred of the other', in short, for a form of 'collective suicide'.

As we have seen, by expressing this type of vote, citizens remove themselves from the circle of reason and morality; being seen as fascist dehumanizes them and makes them into possessed. (A strange accusation, the converse of reality, since the working classes are in reality *dis*possessed.) So why on earth do ordinary people, despite all this, choose apostasy?

Bewitched by this stupid rhetoric of fascism, we never

question the deep motives that lead ordinary people to take the risk of choosing the immorality of a vote in order to express themselves. This transgression is a powerful response to the dominant classes who have been explaining to them for decades that they no longer exist, that they are nothing, that the values they hold are no longer compatible with the 'new world'.

If belief in the existence of the Devil is weakening, this does not herald the end of a discourse that is increasingly based on fear: quite the contrary.

Act II The announcement of dark times

After the Devil come the apocalyptic threats. The end of the world is ubiquitous. Turn on your screens: the planet is exploding, civilizations are dying out, humans are eating each other . . . Thanks to Hollywood, it's as if we were there, in the apocalypse according to Saint Netflix, Saint Amazon and Saint Apple: these are the more or less realistic dystopias broadcast and financed by the multinationals that promote and fuel the model that is taking us there.

Like demonization, this cataclysmic threat blends perfectly into their storytelling, the most striking example being the environmental apocalypse (which is really and truly underway).

The Canadian bio-ecologist William Rees, who originated the concept of the ecological footprint, never ceases to point out the hypocrisy of the ecological discourse of the proponents of a neoliberal model hooked on an eternal growth that is destroying the planet.

> There is no case, in any country, where perpetual growth does not mean a setback for the environment. There is a clear contradiction between continued economic growth and environmental protection. It has always been this way and it will

always be this way. This is an economic model that makes no reference to the environment in general, to biology or to ecosystems, and yet it is the model we use to govern the planet. But it is not possible to have sustainable development if we have an economy whose model takes no account of the system it claims to govern – even though we have already collectively exceeded the ecological capacities of the Earth.[12] The ship is sinking. There are only a few inches left before water rushes into the ship, but we still believe that it is possible to add weight to the vessel.[13]

The effects of the globalized model on the environment are now unarguable. Melting ice, acidification of the oceans, soil contamination, air pollution and the disappearance of thousands of species are now observed, documented and known. But what we also know is that free trade and the exponential growth of maritime and air transport that it brings accelerate the damage. This did not prevent the European Union from signing a brand-new treaty with New Zealand in July 2022. But, rest assured, this ecological aberration of increasing trade with a country located 20,000 kilometres from the European continent is of course part of a commitment by 'both parties to promote sustainable development'.[14]

While unlimited resources are at the heart of the neoliberal project (we would say 'its DNA' today), the proponents of this model are constantly promoting the need for 'sustainable development', that is to say a model of limits. This oxymoron means that the ecological apocalypse that those who are causing it threaten us with is, once again, part of a global narrative. On the other hand, it serves as a justification for tax policies aimed at the ordinary majority (we remember the 'ecological' tax that triggered the Yellow Vest movement), gives political parties the opportunity to capture a new electoral clientele (the younger generations), and allows companies to find new markets with the green business label.

But above all, this exploitation of the apocalyptic threat, at a time when the ruling elites have lost all legitimacy, allows them to annihilate all opposition. From environmental apocalypse to political apocalypse (the threat of fascism) via an apocalypse of healthcare, management by fear allows us to free ourselves from the political realm, and it is all the more effective as it is developing in an aging West. Much more permeable to the media narrative, older populations are, for example, those who most easily give credence to the idea of a fascist threat but also, given their physical fragility, to the sense of a health threat.

Ultimately, this state of anxiety makes it possible to justify the urgency – the urgency to move forward, to keep going, and to reform always at the behest of the market, but without ever gaining the support of the ordinary majority.

Part III
The horizon

The chimeras of a limitless planet, of a successful globalization, of a sustainable metropolization, of a new people, of a perfect algorithm have never succeeded in weakening the working-class fabric. Immune to these battering rams, this solid and now autonomous block even acts like a dike, brutally forcing these fables back on themselves. Supported by the working and middle classes, this irresistible backwash reverses the balance of power.

In the long term, it is the answer to the meaningless model of the market, of the permanent present. Its calm and solidity reveal the hysteria and agitation of the upper strata. It is a return to true (re)sources. We have been deprived of them for half a century, and yet they are infinite: human resources.

However, the new day has not yet dawned, and the world, which has always been chaotic, will remain so. But anchoring ourselves in ordinary reality is opening up a new horizon. The walls of illusion are cracking and the fog is lifting. Slowly, a new prospect is coming into sight, the prospect neither of the trading rooms nor that of the Hollywood sets.

Similar to the sea, this surge is complex, undulating, ungovernable. It can be caused by catastrophic or violent phenomena (in reaction to reforms, social plans, or energy crises), but, in the long term, it is produced mainly by hot or cold currents, visible or invisible, and by phenomena of attraction which are apparently contradictory, but in reality complementary: the social pole and the existential pole. These two forces are generating an unstoppable movement.

7

The radical nature of ordinary life

Sometimes, during an election, a ministerial visit, or a protest movement, the story is interrupted and makes way for the unexpected. Ordinary life emerges from the media fog. An unforeseen event, a spontaneous exchange of views, a simple altercation, and the narrative breaks.

Bruno Le Maire experienced this on 23 February 2018. That day, on the site of the PSA factory in Mulhouse, the Minister of the Economy came 'to assure the French that we will maintain an automobile industry and that the site will remain open'. Half-truth or half-lie, this little sentence exasperated the workers and in particular one trade unionist who, in front of the cameras, did not hesitate to challenge the minister: 'Sir, there were 14,000 of us, there will soon be only 5,000 left in the factory! What will happen to the families?' Stunned by this rather obvious (and legitimate) question, Bruno Le Maire stared into space: his discomfort was palpable. After a few seconds of hesitation, the minister pulled himself together, dodged the question and continued with his vacuous technocratic speech, the kind of thing in which he excels. But it was too late; the day was ruined. It wasn't a good image. Worse, its very absurdity had just illustrated the gap between political narrative and reality.

A few months later, the French President was talking to an unemployed person, who told him that, despite all his attempts, he could not find a job in the horticulture sector. With more aplomb and nerve than the Minister of the Economy, Emmanuel Macron replied that there are jobs in France, in fact it's so easy that 'I only have to cross the street and I'll find you a job.' Going off topic, he continued: 'Go to Montparnasse, the restaurant and café owners there are hiring right now.' This exchange was perceived by the public not only as a denial of reality (according to Pôle Emploi, only six per cent of recruitments are dropped for lack of candidates),[1] since the question of wages and working conditions is never asked, but also as an illustration of the inability to listen and respond to the requests of the less well-off (here's a man who wants to work in a greenhouse, so we talk to him about cafés).

As an impeccable product of the ruling elite, Emmanuel Macron never strays from the frame, he never lets go of the dominant narrative, no matter whom he meets or the reality in front of his eyes. When asked about Seine-Saint-Denis in May 2021, he recited his speech about successful globalization, the world to come, and young start-ups, even stating that 'here, all that's missing to turn us into California is the ocean'.[2] Clearly, it's this overpowering American state (with the fifth largest GDP in the world) with which the inhabitants of this *département* identify, when they leave, or try to leave, this 'promised land'.

More recently, in May 2022, at the Stade de France, which hosted the Champions League final, the spectacle turned grotesque. Faced with the scenes of chaos caused by delinquents, the Minister of the Interior denied what everyone had witnessed, pointing to a ticketing problem and violence caused by British supporters – even though it was the latter who, right in front of the cameras, were the first victims.[3]

If these situations were not so tragic, one could say that the fictional story had reached a completely ludicrous level.

The survival instinct

There is such a gap between the narrative and the reality of the working classes that it makes it impossible for the elites to understand the richness and complexity of what has been bubbling away for twenty years.

Just as the brain remains a mystery, this hidden turmoil has not been recognized. It is in this blind spot that it has developed. This atypical movement draws its strength from a conviction, now shared by the majority, that the dominant narrative is quite vacuous. This observation is not the result of any indoctrination, of an *a priori* refusal of the proposed model, but of a thoughtful analysis, a diagnosis developed over several decades. Contrary to what is systematically asserted, the working classes played the game and tried to live within the framework proposed to them (European, globalized). It was not any ideology that caused the shift, but rather the slow deterioration of their living conditions and the denial of their existence. This cultural non-existence is the driving force of this movement. Existence is its objective. It is in this chaos of emptiness and permanent agitation that the radicalism of ordinary life was born.

Its form, its sociology, its dynamics and its geography distinguish this new movement from all the protests of past centuries.

Unlike the social movements of the nineteenth and twentieth centuries, it is not driven by a struggle for the acquisition of new rights, but by the desire to preserve the social and cultural status of an ordinary majority that was until recently known as the Western middle class. It is not based on the ideology of a future world, but on the desire not to disappear, to exist in today's world. If it does in fact support class interests, those of the least well-off, it goes beyond them. It transcends the 'class struggle' by bringing an existential dimension to it, that of wanting to preserve a meaning to society. It is unique in that it does not aim to create a new world, but to continue it. Autonomous, and long since freed from political, trade union or ideological frameworks, this movement cannot be recuperated.

It is therefore not reducible to the debates that set the camp of the 'progressives' against that of the 'populists', the 'open' world against the 'closed' world. The political events of the last years are, in reality, only epiphenomena – microscopic symptoms of an existential revolt. The election of Donald Trump, the Brexit vote and the dynamics of the National Rally are merely small tremors in a tectonic movement caused by the slow, deliberate displacement of a forgotten continent. The use by the working classes of a few populist puppets is not an ideological endorsement of the promise of a new society, but the expression of a refusal, of the dissipation of the dominant fog. Political time, which has become that of the immediacy of the media and the brevity of elective mandates, is no longer able to capture and even less to recount the long-term framework in which this movement operates.

Driven by an atypical sociology, bringing together working classes of all conditions, origins and statuses (workers, employees, farmers, the self-employed, private and public sector employees, working people, the unemployed, young people, retirees), this reconstituted 'working-class bloc'[4] is something new.

Its geography is also atypical. Regardless of the country in which it emerges (Yellow Vests in France, Brexiteers in Great Britain, 'freedom convoys' in Canada, farmers in the Netherlands),[5] this revolt is rooted in the peripheries, far from the territories that symbolize the neoliberal model, namely the metropolises. Each time, it arouses the same surge of solidarity, the same support in the majority opinion that instinctively recognizes itself in its protests, from which trade unions and political parties are absent. It draws its strength from the violence generated by the loss of the social and cultural status of the ordinary majority; it is not controllable by a narrative composed and handed down from above, and even less can it be 'bought'. You can't buy people who are fighting not only for their purchasing power, but first and foremost to climb out of the existential chaos into which the elites have plunged them.

This ongoing revolt is based above all on disobedience, a cultural disobedience where what is at stake are rather abstract matters.

In Great Britain, the working class, although very materially weakened by deindustrialization, did not in general choose the Labour Party and its redistribution programme, but the liberal-conservative Boris Johnson, who certainly offered a programme of reindustrialization and the revival of public services, but also insisted at length on the preservation of a way of life. Meanwhile, in Hénin-Beaumont, a majority of the unemployed and the poor chose to vote for the National Rally rather than for Mélenchon's La France Insoumise, even though the latter promised a minimum wage of €1,500 net.

Conversely, it is not emphasized enough that the vote of the bourgeoisie, both right and left, and more broadly the vote of the upper classes, is absolutely no longer guided by values, but primarily by concerns about purchasing power and the defence of their heritage.[6]

The electoral hard discount and abstention

From Maoism to wokeism, ordinary people have always observed ideological enthusiasms with great circumspection; but today a real anthropological chasm has opened up. Geographic and cultural separatism is such that it no longer allows the sharing of a minimal base of political or philosophical reference points.

Who can still believe in the existence of a successful globalization, in the solidity of the welfare state and public services, in the excellence of our health and education systems, or in the promise of protecting the environment and strengthening our shared existence?

Can anyone sincerely believe in it? No: nobody.

People are turning away, the conversations in the upper strata are no longer of interest, and election nights have so few viewers that they are now shortened, or even replaced by proper entertainment.[7]

Seemingly indifferent to public affairs, the working classes are invariably condemned and accused of a 'couldn't care less' attitude. When the big bass drum warning of their increasingly fascist tendencies is not being beaten, it is replaced by the quieter background music of indifference and withdrawal into oneself. The levels of abstention seem to prove the lack of interest in the common good. At each election, the same old story. By voting 'badly' and especially by abstaining, the less well-off are deemed to be displaying their profound lack of attention to others and to society. This distressing picture hides a particular detail: the way the electoral supply is adapted to the demand of the upper classes. This supply of 'Professional Security Agreement Plus' has continued to expand to the detriment of the 'working-class' supply. Liberal, environmentalist, right or left, young or old, wealthy voters will always find what they are looking for on the increasingly gentrified market of politics.

In the same way that the Parisian department stores have gradually abandoned the segment catering for middle and working-class categories,[8] the electoral market has specialized in the high end. The working-class majority, who have understood that they aren't going to find anything affordable there, no longer frequent the market, or do so less and less; those among them who still consume politics tend to go towards the low-end 'populist' brands, the hard discounts of the sector.[9]

In most elections, a majority of the working classes abstains. This betokens less an indifference to public affairs (a depoliticization) than the fact that they realise they have been dispossessed of their sovereignty. To vote or not to vote, that is not the question. In reality, ordinary people are hardly more interested in contemporary political debate than in subsidized French cinema that only films itself, forgetting the sociological majority of the country. This doesn't mean that they don't like cinema! Abstention illustrates the empowerment of the working classes, not their withdrawal. The absurd idea that they have deliberately chosen to withdraw into their private sphere is typical of an over-generalized, out-of-touch analysis, one that omits an essential point. First, individualism is above all an ideology; and, furthermore, ordinary people do not have the means for this individualism. Their lives are governed by the forced solidarities of daily lives adversely affected by their low incomes, diminishing the social and immaterial capital they absolutely need to survive.

Attachment to the commons, to public services, to the welfare state, to the sovereign state has never wavered. Why? Because people know full well that they do not have the means, unlike the upper classes, to be treated in private clinics, to send their children to private schools or to entrust their security to private bodyguards. They are grappling with a radicalism quite beyond the ken of armchair experts.

And, in the middle classes, radicalism is cool. 'Disruptive' postures, revolutionary exaltations, speeches that 'turn the tables' have always excited the bourgeoisie. In 2017, Emmanuel Macron called the book in which he set forth his programme *Revolution*.

From the rebellocrats of the film set to the screenwriters of the entertainment industry, subversion is promoted, celebrated, encouraged and controlled. But, if there is one form of radicalism that people are wary of, it is the radicalism of the ordinary majority, who don't play at being cardboard rebels but foster the real subversion of ordinary life, the complete opposite of the dominant model.

This radicalism, this autonomous movement, is the product of a daily struggle. And, contrary to what the zeitgeist sings, it does not contrast 'the end of the month' with the 'end of the world' (yet another narrative imagined by the elites who suggest a rivalry between losers and poets), but points to the difference between the market and life itself; it sets those who feed us the illusory story of a benevolent model, while protecting themselves from its harmful effects against those who have to confront true otherness, the social otherness of an increasingly inegalitarian and precarious system, as well as cultural otherness. This otherness, promoted but never experienced by the elites, lies behind the great existential movement of the working classes.

8

Not against but elsewhere

Impervious to the harangues of those who dispossess them, ordinary people have started an uprising whose springs are mainly immaterial.

This is not a call for help addressed to our leaders, but an existential call aimed at society itself. Its singularity is that it is not based on any ideology, but on a primary, vital force, produced by the fundamental experience of existence, of a daily struggle that allows people to confront reality with energy and not with systems. Based on an original act of rebellion ('*no* to the dominant narrative'), this movement cannot be reduced to the narrow frameworks of technocratic analysis. Without regard for the moralism of the present time, ordinary people have, in a few short decades, shaped the cultural base, the fulcrum, on which to rebuild a model that would finally make sense.

At each election, at each surge of social fever, the 'soothsayers of the République',[1] as Jacques Julliard calls them – researchers, experts, journalists and pollsters – are on deck to explain to us what the French meant. 'On election night, the field no longer belongs to the voter but to the commentariat [...] wearing a deerstalker hat and armed with an enormous magnifying glass, or better still, the bowler hat and pipe of Commissioner Maigret.' And Julliard puts his finger on an essential point when he recalls that 'until the eve of the Second World War, it was up to elected officials to decipher and give meaning to the monosyllabic oracles falling from the mouth of the Sibyl'.[2] 'This unbearable closed-door meeting' is the fruit of a long process that has seen the technocrat replace the politician, the trend chart replace the majority, and marketing figures replace the existential dimension. The recurring and endless debates that consist of guessing whether the priority of voters is 'purchasing power', 'the environment', 'insecurity' or 'immigration' are typical of this drift.

The fundamental question lies elsewhere. But is this 'elsewhere' still within the reach of a political class that has now gone over entirely to business management? In this microcosm, any mention of an immaterial movement creates at best incomprehension, at worst indifference, and always sneering. But could it be otherwise?

How could a force that brings together all the dimensions of existence (from the social to the cultural, from the economic to the political, from the material to the spiritual) be reduced to the algorithmic vision of the economics ministry technocrats and the BETC admen?[3] How can we describe what 'is' to the apostles of change for the sake of change?[4]

We're not going to agree with Jacques Julliard here, plonk Sherlock's deerstalker or Maigret's bowler hat on our heads, and stride off to investigate. Let's leave the magnifying glass and the pipe to others, let's simply try to recall what makes ordinary life rich and radical. Such a life is not part of a modelled future, but rather a complex and ambivalent reality, which the robots that govern us cannot grasp.

How we label this protest – 'social', left, far left or Marxist, for some, and 'identitarian', right, far right or Maurrassian[5] for others – seems impossible. We are not facing a remake of the peasant revolts of the Middle Ages, nor of the workers' movements of the 1930s, nor of the revolution of May '68, but rather of the novelty of a movement in which the questions of the 'end of the month' and the 'end of the world' are intertwined.

The protest of ordinary people in different countries no longer belongs to those who have forgotten them and pushed them aside. Nor does it belong to politicians, or trade unions, or the world of culture, or the intelligentsia. Nor does it belong to a camp, neither to the left, nor to the right, nor to the extremes. Nor does it embrace the comfy 'old-fashioned class struggle' born of a conscious conflict of social categories that are economically and culturally integrated and therefore politically represented. It does not fit into any pre-established sociological or ideological framework.

The various categories of the working classes do not share a 'class consciousness', but something more powerful: their common destiny. They have forged a solid diagnosis of the effects of the economic and societal model imposed on them. They have not hardened themselves through class-based social struggles, but 'thanks to' the cultural ostracization to which they are subjected.

For the first time, the ordinary majority is not 'against' the spectacle of an impotent political power, but 'elsewhere'. And this positioning, outside social struggles and the social consciousness being kept under control, destabilizes this very control.

A dialogue of the deaf

Unable to understand the profound nature of the protest, political power seeks to reduce it to themes that are easily 'demonized', for example by highlighting the vote for populist parties or the violence of certain demonstrations. These trivial subjects, whose sole objective is to fuel the narrative of fear through the media, fail to capture the quiet strength of people who are not fighting against a fictitious power but for their very existence.

The lack of understanding of the nature of this movement was harshly revealed during the Yellow Vest crisis. Experts, consultants and politicians[6] asked people to present their programme, to answer multiple choice questions, to choose between 'purchasing power' and 'lifestyle', to explain with figures and 'concrete' demands what they were asking for. How much did they need? How much should be written on the cheques? Did they want a universal basic income? While the strength of this revolt lay precisely in the fact that it never proposed easy solutions to all these questions, people simply answered 'we just want to exist'.

This transcendence is intellectually very striking. Irreducible to PowerPoint presentations and Excel spreadsheets, this movement is terrifying, because it does not just talk about purchasing power but about every dimension of existence. The social issue for ordinary people is filling their shopping cart, but it is above all about fulfilling themselves in their work, and being respected in their social life.

Western powers completely fail to grasp this: they think, like the totalitarian regimes before them (in the USSR, for example, people were fed, housed, cared for), that it is enough to ensure the 'material' dimension to create a viable (and even enviable) society. From now on, all crises are managed with billions. 'Big' politics comes down to one thing: printing money, distributing money and increasing debt. This materialistic headlong rush finds its peak in a project promoted for years by the liberal elites of Davos,[7] Silicon Valley and the bourgeois left (the expression is starting to become a pleonasm): universal income. Once again, there is a total lack of understanding between, on the one hand, ordinary people who are fighting to regain their place and their dignity, and, on the other, the ruling classes who reduce this fight to a budget line.

The working classes are not asking for charity, but for a properly paid job, regulated by law, which offers them security. It should be remembered that social existence is guaranteed by access to a (social) function, not to (social) benefits, to welfare.

While it reveals a profound lack of understanding of the rejection, on the part of the least well-off, of what is called 'benefit' (which they do not confuse with the welfare state), universal income constitutes the ultimate epilogue of the long process of their exclusion. After several decades of social destruction, it marks the beginning of the era of dependency.

This project reveals the fundamentally materialist perception of the 'elite bloc',[8] for whom the social role of the working classes now resides solely in consumption. It is no coincidence that the theme of 'purchasing power' is gradually replacing that of work. It offers technocrats the opportunity to give a social veneer to a project that is devastating society and thus to showcase its benevolence, its care for the weakest, and its desire to redistribute 'whatever the cost'.[9]

Presented as 'generous and supportive', this policy is first and foremost – as people so often forget to point out – the consequence of a model that has destroyed industrial employment. It also helps to pass off over-indebtedness (and therefore the submission of states to banks) as the consequence of an overly generous welfare state (and therefore excessive social demands from the working classes). However, if social needs are important, it is first and foremost because the economic model supported by the elites has failed to create enough jobs, and especially stable, properly paid jobs. This accusatory inversion is all the more perverse as it will soon be used to justify an increase in the (direct or indirect) taxation of the ordinary majority to pay this debt.

Note that the same rhetoric is used when elected officials and residents of peripheral France denounce the withdrawal of public services,[10] always set against the size of transfers (social benefits, civil servant salaries and even retirement pensions).

In this dialogue of the deaf, some speak of a palpable reality, that of a relationship with the state and of the place of working-class France in the economic model, while others refer to the liberal theory of trickle-down. Here again, the basic issues – deindustrialization, the hardship of work, and wage stagnation – are hidden. The existence of this France is limited to wage adjustment.

The working classes are reduced, from this perspective – the perspective of an accountant – to an anomic mass whose life can be summed up by the articles piled up in their shopping carts. And this is how a sated bourgeoisie reassures itself, by making them pass for imbeciles whose horizon is limited to that: filling shopping carts. The attack was also carried out during the Yellow Vests crisis: the system's foot soldiers were endlessly surprised by the material comfort of the demonstrators who bought useless products (flat screens, smartphones), or even, scandalously, branded products.[11] This refrain was nothing new: for centuries, the bourgeoisie had suggested that if the poor were poor, it was first and foremost because they were unable to manage their budgets. ('You're poor? Just stop.')

This underhanded representation of working-class society to the tune of 'They've never had it so good!' is all the more indecent because it is endorsed by social categories that overconsume, and for whom it is fashionable to mock and judge the level of consumption of those who have to keep a close eye on what they spend.[12]

In any case, this 'working-class equals consumer' idea is absolutely untrue. In June 2022, the Ipsos institute confirmed that the budgetary room for manoeuvre of the French had continued to decline, and that these days 58 per cent of them have to budget for shopping with a margin of €10 or less![13] The survey also emphasized that a majority made 'selected savings' on so-called 'secondary' needs, such as outings and cultural products (60% of cases), clothing (56%) and high-tech products (54%). And now, 66 per cent of people wait until products are on special offer before they can buy them. This is far removed from the eternal bourgeois representation of the poor who are unable to manage their budgets. This is in any case hardly surprising, given the low disposable income. The Ipsos institute also estimates that the average shopping basket is €377 per month per family (a couple and two children), for daily shopping. Far, very far from a working-class France that's busy filling its face! The consumer society as the horizon of the ordinary majority? Really? It's not consumption that sets the pace for the daily lives of ordinary people, but social insecurity caused by the lack of employment and low income; a social tension felt strongly by those who live far from the most active areas of employment.[14]

And what about a summit conference on living conditions?

As well as this social insecurity, there are physical and cultural insecurities. For the working classes, the spread of insecurity is one of the major signs of a deterioration in their way of life. In this area, the failure of the state is perceived at best as proof of a real downgrading, and at worst as abandonment. The explosion of violence against people, the proliferation of neighbourhoods controlled by traffickers, and the spread of delinquency throughout the country[15] have shattered a framework essential to ordinary people: the control of public space. In the working-class imagination, 'the street' is not only a place of passage, it is also the place where people exist, where they communicate, where they are respected. By allowing insecurity to set in, the ruling classes have deprived the less well-off of the place where they can exercise their social capital.

This failure is experienced as a negation of their existence: it underlines the place of 'those who are nothing', those who don't have the means to move or protect themselves.

The cultural insecurity that weakens this way of life is linked to the failure of the state in one of its sovereign missions: the regulation of migratory flows.

Here again, the working classes make a majority, ultra-majority diagnosis. Whatever their social origins and places of residence (from rural areas to the sensitive suburbs of large cities), the less well-off categories are waiting for only one thing: for the state to take its responsibilities.

After having lost their status as an 'economic and social reference point', the working and middle classes have been dispossessed of their status as a 'cultural reference point', which until recently still operated for the elites as well as for new arrivals. By losing this status, ordinary people (whatever their origins) see their cultural existence contested from above *and* from below.

The defence of a protective way of life is not the prerogative of a few dismayed rednecks: it is an invariant, a survival instinct common to the whole working class, including those who live in immigrant neighbourhoods. Immersed in the multicultural model of large metropolises, the immigrant working classes protect themselves by opposing it with the cultural coherence of their own value system. Unlike the 'old' immigrants who arrived before the 1980s, the new ones settle in spaces where they no longer have, right before their eyes, the majority reference point of the 'traditional' working classes. Assimilation to a common and working-class base is therefore no longer possible. As they do not recognize themselves in the cultural bath of the metropolitan bourgeoisie either, the new immigrant working classes are therefore attached to a protective lifestyle based on imported values. If the excesses of this model are known (communitarianism, Islamization, a counter-society), it is not sufficiently emphasized that the deep-rooted motivation of the majority of the inhabitants of these neighbourhoods is first and foremost to defend their protective cultural base against the dominant model of the big cities. If the metropolitan model is perfectly adapted to a bourgeoisie that has the means to preserve itself (socially and culturally), it creates major cultural insecurity within these immigrant working classes. Attachment to traditions, religion, and even the flag (which we see emerging at every opportunity in the heart of globalized metropolises, even though nationalism is proscribed in them), are all signs of their (universal) desire to preserve their protective cultural capital.

In the suburbs, as in peripheral France, it will take much more than a summit conference on living conditions to 'settle' this protest movement among the working classes. It will take no less than a change of model.

It is decidedly 'elsewhere', this protest; it has taken a radical step aside, and it produces a much more fundamental and serious critique than a revolution that is kept under control. Ultimately, it is a response to 'the empire of the lesser evil',[16] the liberal society that had excluded from the public space any reference to the idea of common morality. By putting it back at the centre of things, the existential movement of ordinary people is paving the way for an implosion.

9

Return to the centre

It is not because protest is based on a fundamentally moral, i.e. just, phenomenon, that it will prevail. We can hope that, after a series of defeats, victory lies at the end of the road: but, to paraphrase Charles Péguy, 'virtue has clean hands, but it has no hands'.[1] The 'elite bloc' is neither defeated nor has it been replaced, simply weakened; but its days are numbered, the social and political movements of recent years being only preludes to the gathering storm – especially since there is a process that inevitably works against it: that of the self-destruction of the model.

As if in a mirror image, we are witnessing the self-destruction of the ruling elites themselves. In order to satisfy their desire for power, wealth and control, they have signed a Faustian pact (abandoning the common good, society, the majority) and, by the same token, set going a timer that they can no longer stop. Their future is suspended by a 'piece of shagreen'. As in the novel, they are not particularly concerned about the diabolical warning: 'your wishes will be accurately fulfilled, but at the expense of your life'.[2] Inevitably, as they build up their political, cultural, and financial successes, the circle of their days, as represented by this skin, shrinks. And, like the Balzacian hero

Raphaël de Valentin, they imagine themselves to be in charge of a model that will never die.

The idiot

This stubbornness, this intellectual narrowness, this stupidity are so widespread that we can speak of an idiocracy.[3] Nassim Nicholas Taleb was one of the first to evoke this ridiculous figure, typical of modernity: the 'intellectual yet idiot'. This is the expression that the researcher came up with for 'that class of paternalistic semi-intellectual experts with some Ivy league, Oxford–Cambridge, or similar label-driven education who are telling the rest of us (1) what to do, (2) what to eat, (3) how to speak, (4) how to think . . . and (5) who to vote for'.[4] He has identified the fact that, the more visible the decline in the intellectual and cultural level of the 'elites' becomes, the more they ostracize the lower classes.

This decline, particularly obvious to anyone who pays the slightest attention to Western political life, actually affects most elites. For example, in their report on the 2017 entrance exam, ENA[5] juries pointed out these declines in level: the answers to exam questions were all the same, the candidates were unable to produce 'an original idea, to think for themselves',[6] and their conformism was such that they 'stammer[ed] out one and the same idea, while showing themselves incapable of thinking in a more personal way'. Already fifty years earlier, in a scathing essay, Jean-Pierre Chevènement called out the members of the 'enarchy': they were the 'mandarins of bourgeois society'.[7] The ENA itself now emphasizes that heads full of mere information, sometimes 'incapable of putting things into perspective, or even understanding them', and not always even able to spell, now aspire to presiding over the country's destiny. This focus on 'the enarchy' is representative of the upper strata of society at the end of their tether. Its products struggle to argue logically, cannot recognize a reality that goes beyond their own limits, submit to a dictatorship of emotion and to a silly notion of political correctness, and lack all discernment. These days, the fake elite hardly takes anyone in, and that is why it never ceases to turn the stigma around and to emphasize even more the potentially destructive stupidity of the less well-off.[8]

This decline in cultural and intellectual level, a decline that underlies the loss of meaning in politics, is automatically heightening the emphasis on technocratic and communicational know-how, one that now permeates all areas of news, culture, education, and research. Hiding stupidity behind their degrees, the smug representation of a society divided between 'educated', overqualified people (the lack of a degree, read as 'stupidity', is systematically seen as a mainstay of the populist vote) and non- or poorly qualified people (plebs) is the life insurance of the dominant classes. The problem is that, if it is effective in shutting down the debate, this representation simply accelerates their intellectual confinement.

The ruling classes of Western countries are blind and deaf, and also powerless – a powerlessness that they have patiently organized and manufactured, first by handing over politics to supranational technocratic bodies, then by abandoning themselves to the banks and, consequently, by causing the debt to explode. Illegitimate in the eyes of public opinion, without real economic and political power, their world is self-destructing before our eyes.

Deglobalization is underway. It can be measured. While, for almost forty years (1980–2017), international trade grew twice as fast as global GDP (according to INSEE, the former grew by a factor of 6.8 and the latter by 3.5), the movement has since been reversed.[9] The WTO predicted that, in 2022, global production would increase faster than trade. Trade is now increasingly focused on services and less and less on goods. This observation reflects a gradual relocation of productive activity that has become vital for many Western countries.

The totemic organization of the upper strata around the triptych of globalization/free trade/metropolitanization is floundering. Some of the elites no longer believe in it. There are even apostates on the flagship in the United States, in a group above all suspicion: the so-called progressive ruling class. While Donald Trump had accustomed us to the critique of free trade and the need to relocate industries, the statement by the Treasury Secretary of the Biden administration in April 2022 came as a surprise: Janet Yellen, who is also a brilliant economist, indirectly announced the death of globalization by talking about friendshoring; in other words, she invented the oxymoron of 'globalization among friends'. In essence: 'In the future, it will be increasingly difficult to separate economic issues from broader considerations of national interest, including national security.'[10] Deglobalization, the promotion of short supply chains, and the priority of national interests are moving centre stage: the dominant model is gradually losing its substance. While there is no doubt that, like a Dostoyevskian hero,[11] a fraction of the elite will become aware of the insignificance and danger of the model, it will be a while before the penny drops. The more weakened and illegitimate they appear, the more the ruling classes seem to display their arrogance and complacency. They no longer speak: they preach, moralize, and display their self-satisfaction. Still borne by their inertia, the dominant model continues sailing blindly on. In the West, where more words (and more debt) are produced than goods, it resembles a ship of fools.

The West doesn't need anyone else's help to decline

There has never been so much talk about the end of the West. Not a day, not a week goes by without some intellectual mentioning the end of this civilizational bloc. Propounded by the neoconservative camp, this theme is not new, since it was in

1918, in the context of the self-destruction of Europe, that Oswald Spengler published his polemical text, *The Decline of the West*.[12] In this metaphysical essay, the German philosopher set out his cyclical conception of civilizations and cultures that live through their childhood, their youth, their maturity and their old age. A century later, Régis Debray expressed surprise that the word 'West', which in the twentieth century 'had a whiff of the diabolical', is now commonly used, even by progressive intellectuals.[13] This resurgence was fostered by the century's great debate, between Francis Fukuyama, who announced the 'end of History', and Samuel Huntington's 'clash of civilizations'.[14]

Fukuyama's text, published after the fall of the Berlin Wall and the collapse of the Soviet Empire, announced the victory of Western values. Conversely, Huntington's text emphasized the emergence of potentially conflicting civilizational blocs. For Hubert Védrine, for example, the end of History was in fact less Fukuyama's subject than that of the 'rebirth of a liberal optimism after the century and the fall of totalitarian regimes'.[15] And today, the former Minister of Foreign Affairs of the French Socialist government of the 1990s[16] recognizes that it was Huntington who was 'unfortunately not wrong', that the world we live in resembles less Fukuyama's than Huntington's. If the West has dominated the world for three or four centuries, other countries now want to take their revenge by rejecting the 'evangelization' that accelerated with the end of the Soviet Union, notably under the banner of 'Human Rights'. The Western monopoly in the conduct of economic and geopolitical affairs has had its day. The world has become multipolar and is de-Westernizing itself: witness the dynamism of the BRICS and the lethargy of the G7 countries.[17]

Conversely, the economic dynamism of emerging countries, as well as the demographic growth of Muslim and African worlds, illuminate the loss of vitality and decline in the West. This theme of exhaustion is no longer the preserve of a few

Cassandras or neo-cons, but permeates a large part of public opinion. Against a backdrop of ecological collapse, there are increasing signs of a Western endgame: economic backwardness, deindustrialization, de-dollarization,[18] over-indebtedness, the ageing of the population, the intensification of migratory flows, and the crisis of the school and university systems. At the end of this inevitable process, the risk of annihilation is becoming clearer. Between those who analyse it objectively and those who deplore it, this picture suffers from a major oversight on the part of everyone – the exclusion of those who keep civilization going, with its values and its internal dynamics: ordinary people. Because, if 'the history of Western Europe is a willed destiny',[19] it is clear that, by excluding the working classes, it is the ruling elites who have broken this destiny, and the other civilizational blocs have little to do with it.

In other words, the West must take responsibility for its own annihilation.

In reality, it needs neither China, nor Islam, nor global warming in order to disappear. It can manage this all by itself. It is less external powers, ideologies or religions that are destroying Western countries than a process of self-destruction that is depriving them of their vital springs and their defences. This self-destruction of the economy, of common values, of the way of life has little to do with India, the Middle East or the ageing of the population,[20] but everything to do with the abandonment of ordinary society – the ultimate system error.

By ejecting it from the matrix, the ruling elites have destroyed the cultural base that embodies and sustains the values of any civilization. The removal to the geographical and cultural peripheries of those who carry forward this system of values is the start of the process of devitalization and then decivilization. Preferring to look away from this original bug in the system, we blame the outside, the others.

How can we imagine 'saving' a civilization by leaving by the wayside those who carry forward and sustain on a daily basis the values and the way of life that it has produced? Today, Western societies do not need a 'war of civilizations', for which they no longer have the means or, above all, the desire, but a social electroshock that would respond not only to the widespread lament, but also to the programmed annihilation.

In his latest novel,[21] Michel Houellebecq evokes the slowdown and immobilization of the West as preludes to its annihilation.

The remedy is a return to its human resources.

The long chronicle of blindness has almost reached its epilogue. The magic of the three tales that compose it ('no alternative', 'no society', 'no majority') no longer casts its spell. The pied pipers are increasingly playing out of tune, and the enthusiastic crowd that followed them yesterday has been transformed into a ramshackle march of zombies continuing to lurch after powerless elites, whose days are numbered.

Should we, alongside the tellers of fairy-tales, continue the adventure towards a programmed chaos, or anchor ourselves again in reality, with ordinary society? Should we prolong the agony with the possessed, or rebuild the world with the dispossessed? In reality, we are not faced with a choice, but with a necessity. Placed for too long on the periphery of the world, the ordinary majority *must* return to the centre.

Unsurprisingly, this return to the centre will be hotly contested. The haughty intelligentsia will explain to us that the world is too complex to be carried forward by people who are not sufficiently educated – that the life of deplorables cannot represent a model. Ah, how distant is the time when one could be amused by the fact that 'two intellectuals sitting down go less far than a brute who walks'![22] This joke dates from the height of the *Trente Glorieuses*, exactly the period when the ordinary majority, economically integrated and still culturally and politically dominant, was at the 'centre'.

The question is no longer to come up with a diagnosis or to ponder what has caused it all: it's been perfectly obvious for a long time. The heated debates are just a way to give a bit of sparkle to the show and keep it going. Only experts and politicians continue to discuss the evils and the 'solutions': in the real world, everyone's already got the message. The challenge is now to emerge, once and for all, from the fog of unreality. To do this, we only have to take the path that was once called the sovereignty of the people.

This return to the centre is not a return to the past, but an anchoring in contemporary reality. It is not about revisiting the lost world of the working class, but on the contrary, relying on those who, against all odds, have continued to take charge of social and cultural realities and to preserve a common good and values that surpass and precede all ideologies and all systems.

It's now okay to be pragmatic

The utopia of a model freed from the constraints of ordinary life is coming to an end. Despite attempts at enslavement, this crazy project has not succeeded in destroying the survival instinct of those who have always carried society forward. It is by relying on this survival instinct and on their pragmatism that we will be able to envisage reconstruction. This return to reality would allow us, in a few years (decades?), not to solve all the problems, but at least to ease tensions, to reassure ordinary people about their future, to reaffirm their place in the economy and their status as a cultural reference.

Since the Covid crisis, reindustrialization, support for certain strategic relocations, the endogenous development of territories and even the idea of a form of protectionism are once again perceived as rational objectives. Indeed, part of the ruling elite recently 'discovered' that pragmatism is not forbidden in economics and pointed out the need to recover a form of sovereignty in this area. For the first time since the 1980s, some elites have realized this obvious fact: we cannot base an economy and therefore a society on a model that produces nothing.

In cultural and societal fields, pragmatism is not forbidden either. The Scandinavian countries have demonstrated that in this area, it is possible to calm tensions by responding to the demands of ordinary people. But, to initiate measures, the Danish or Swedish elites had first to carry out their intellectual revolution, to realize that they were not in office to serve utopias, but to serve the majority.

It is by thinking against themselves that the Danish elites have radically revised their migration policy. Opening their eyes to the development of cultural tensions, separatism, and the ghettoization of certain neighbourhoods and schools, they have revised downwards their philosophy of openness, implementing for example their 'anti-ghetto' policy. These pragmatic measures have certain political effects: supported by a majority of public opinion and by the political class, and carried forward by social democrats, they have broken the dynamic of the extreme right parties.

On the other side of the Øresund Bridge, which connects Copenhagen to Malmö, the Swedish Democrats have also been caught up in reality. In 2000, Sweden, which defined itself as a 'moral superpower', encouraged the reception of migratory flows that have since become exponential. It is clear that, for ten years, cultural tensions, riots, and ghettoization have hit the country.[23] As in Denmark, the Swedish elites, including on the left, have looked reality in the face and also changed their minds, accepting the idea that there were objective thresholds for reception. In 2020, it was a social-democratic government that decided to reduce entries.

It should be noted that this pragmatism does not apply solely to the migration issue. In 2021, Sweden again, although a pioneer in this area, reversed its policy facilitating sex changes for minors.[24]

If pragmatism is still considered by the ruling elites to be an unbearable submission to reality, it allows us to break economic and societal decisions, and various dogmas, which have turned out to cause more damage than positive effects.[25] Now, the demands of the majority can be met. Pragmatism is opposed to utopian idealism. It is the search for the 'least worst' kind of reality and not an ideal world.

Epilogue

After the Covid pandemic, the ideology of metropolitanization imploded.[1] Today, it is giving way to elected officials, who take a much more pragmatic attitude to regional planning. On this point, the working classes benefit from a capital that the upper classes do not have; they live far from the 'hell of big cities'[2] in spaces which, if they succeed in producing their own wealth and jobs, are best suited to the coming urban and ecological transition.

The way the territories of peripheral France are viewed is changing. They are increasingly perceived as a potential, a solution to the economic impasse. In the wake of the geographer Gérard-François Dumont,[3] a fraction of the elites now think that small towns, medium-sized towns, and the countryside offer the conditions for endogenous and sustainable development, because all these territories have one inestimable force: human resources. At the beginning, there are ordinary people, artisans, farmers, and traders, who carry forward an idea, a project that makes sense locally (a policy adapted to their geography), and in the end it is a small sustainable economy based on short supply chains and a spirit of solidarity that is taking shape. This return to the human (re)source is not only the condition for the development of these territories, it also marks a halt to the process of dispossession, the annihilation of individual lives and of society as a whole.

The return of ordinary people to the centre is the only answer to the threat of chaos, and the only condition for reconstruction.

This anchoring in ordinary reality will not lead us to a perfect world, but (and this will already be a great deal) to a world that will have meaning. This is now the only horizon.

THERE IS AN ALTERNATIVE.

Notes

1 Access to the sea

1 The CGT (Confédération Générale du Travail or General Confederation of Labour) is a confederation of French trades unions. The Confédération générale de la production française (General Federation of French Production) was an association of French employers. (Translator's note.)
2 Marc Boyer, *Histoire du tourisme de masse* (Paris: PUF, 1999).
3 The *Trente Glorieuses* were the Thirty Glorious Years from 1945–75, a period in which France recovered from the Second World War and enjoyed economic growth. (Translator's note.)
4 The Front de libération de la Bretagne is a clandestine Breton independence organization created in 1966. With its armed branch, the ARB (Breton Revolutionary Army), it calls for the reunification of Brittany, and its independence.
5 'Le retour du Front de libération de la Bretagne', *Le Télégramme*, 27 June 2022.
6 According to INSEE (the French national office for statistics), the number of secondary residences increased 3.6-fold on the Breton coast between 1968 and 2018. At the same time, the number of seasonal rental advertisements exploded, creating unprecedented real-estate tensions.

7 The *Fronte di liberazione nazionale di a Corsica* (Corsican National Liberation Front) is a radical Corsican independence movement created in 1976.
8 *Insee Première*, no. 1871, August 2021.
9 A *zone tendue* is an area where there is a housing shortage. (Translator's note.)
10 'Pays basque: un tsunami Airbnb', *Le Figaro*, 8 June 2022.
11 'Bretagne: quand les Parisiens raflent l'immobilier', *L'Obs*, 13 August 2021.
12 'La révolte des villes touristiques contre le système Airbnb', *Le Figaro*, 9 June 2022.
13 'Spéculation foncière en Corse', *Corse Matin*, 6 February 2022.
14 'La révolte des villes touristiques contre le système Airbnb', *Le Soir*, 12 June 2022.
15 Branko Milanović, *Inégalités mondiales: le destin des classes moyennes* (Paris: La Découverte, 2021).
16 In French, *le monde d'en haut* (literally 'the world [of] above'). In the English translation of Guilluy's *Le crépuscule de la France d'en haut*, the phrase is translated as 'the elites': see Christophe Guilluy, *Twilight of the Elites: Prosperity, the Periphery, and the Future of France*, translated by Malcolm DeBevoise (New Haven, CT and London: Yale University Press, 2019). However, as Guilluy also frequently uses the French term *élites* (here 'elites'), I have here preferred to translate *le monde d'en haut* as 'the upper strata'. (Translator's note.)
17 Source: CRÉDOC, data for 2019.
18 Including on the popular beaches of the *département* of the Somme.
19 Accessible old private housing stock, i.e. low-rent, low-cost houses or apartments.
20 As a reminder, it was precisely to break this irenic vision of gentrification that I have previously hijacked David Brooks' term 'bobo'. The aim was to designate the 'gentrifier' on the basis of his or her class position, that of a new bourgeoisie.
21 The adjective 'unbowed' (*insoumise*) is an allusion to the left-wing

political party La France Insoumise (France Unbowed), founded in 2016 by Jean-Luc Mélenchon. (Translator's note.)
22 The pro-independence collective Dispac'h focuses on putting up posters on unoccupied houses in the Saint-Malo region.
23 Hovig Ter Minassian, 'Patrimonialisation et gentrification: Le cas de Barcelone', *Cahier Construction politique et sociale des territoires*, 2012, pp. 49–58.
24 'La gentrification du quartier de Shoreditch', *RFI*, October 2015. (This attack on the Cereal Killer cafe was carried out by anti-gentrification activists on 26 September 2015. – Translator's note.)
25 Peripheral France is the term used by Guilluy to refer to the (mainly rural) areas of France that have been neglected by the political elite. (Translator's note.)

2 The forbidden city
1 'Gilets jaunes, l'exemple des mutations de Bordeaux et de la Gironde', *Le Figaro*, 21 November 2018.
2 'C'est la première fois que l'on voit émerger ces tensions sociales en Gironde', *20 minutes*, 11 December 2018.
3 *The Prisoner* was a dystopian British television series broadcast from 1967.
4 The notion of a 'metropolitan archipelago' was introduced by geographer Olivier Dollfus in 1994.
5 Between 2006 and 2016, employment growth was concentrated in nine large metropolises (*Insee Première*, no. 1771, 2019).
6 Guillaume Faburel, *Les Métropoles barbares* (Paris: Le Passager clandestin, 2019).
7 The Beurs march began in October 1983; SOS Racisme was created in 1984. (The Beurs are French people whose parents or grandparents were born in the Maghreb; SOS Racisme, an anti-racist organization, was founded in France but has counterparts in other European countries. – Translator's note.)
8 Jean-Claude Michéa, *L'Empire du moindre mal* (Paris: Champs Flammarion, 2021).

9 Christophe Guilluy, 'Les bobos vont faire mal', *Libération*, 8 January 2001.
10 Programme Action cœur de ville, ministère de la Cohésion des territoires et des Relations avec les collectivités territoriales, 19 July 2022, https://www.cohesionterritoires.gouv.fr/programme-action-cœur-de-ville.
11 That was how Emmanuel Macron, President of the Republic, put it in 2018 ('Look at social policy: we're putting a crazy amount of cash into social benefits, people are still poor').
12 As stated by Benjamin Griveaux, government spokesperson, in 2018.
13 In 2016, 57 per cent of senior executives were members of an association compared to 33 per cent of workers and 35 per cent of employees. Source: INSEE.
14 According to the OECD, it takes six generations to move from the working class to the middle class.
15 In 2016, children from very privileged backgrounds made up 73 per cent of the students at Sciences Po Paris or the École Normale Supérieure on Rue d'Ulm, 89 per cent of those at Hautes Études Commerciales and 92 per cent of those at the École Polytechnique; children from modest backgrounds made up less than eight per cent of the students at these schools. (These are all highly competitive and prestigious institutions of higher education. – Translator's note.)
16 Christophe Guilluy, 'La France périphérique délaissée', *Libération*, 1 October 2003.
17 Christophe Guilluy, *No Society. La fin de la classe moyenne occidentale* (Paris: Flammarion, 2018), p. 70.
18 'La géographie de l'ascension sociale', *France Stratégie*, no. 36, November 2015.
19 Michaël Sicsic, INSEE, 19 May 2022.
20 Christophe Guilluy, *Fractures françaises* (Paris: Flammarion, 2013).
21 'White working-class boys in England "need more help" to go to university', *Guardian*, 10 May 2018.

22 Salomé Berlioux and Erkki Maillard, *Les Invisibles de la République: comment sauver la jeunesse de la France périphérique* (Paris: J'ai Lu, 2020).
23 The president of the Chemins d'avenirs association gives the striking example of a class of middle-school students located forty minutes from Grenoble, more than half of whose students have never even been there.

3 The social imprint

1 This was the slogan of François Hollande's 2012 campaign.
2 The 'Hero of the Scientific Union' geneticist Trofim Denisovich Lysenko dominated biology in the Soviet Empire during Stalin's reign by promising to save agriculture with theories that would prove absurd. To assert himself, he stifled all scientific debate by ostracizing his opponents and arresting or executing eminent scientists. Lysenko's vague theories contaminated scientific circles in Western Europe, particularly in France. Since then, the term Lysenkoism has come to refer by extension to a science corrupted by ideology, where facts are concealed or interpreted in a scientifically erroneous manner.
3 'It has no name, no face, no party. It will never run for office. It will not be elected. My real adversary is the world of finance.' Speech by François Hollande at Le Bourget, 22 January 2012.
4 Global Inequality Report 2022, World Inequality Lab.
5 The denunciation of the one per cent has become the great specialty of the left-wing bourgeoisie. As the expert avant-garde of the subsidized rebellocracy (subsidized by the state or the big multinationals via the think-tanks), this left has just been baptized by Jean-Claude Michéa the 'ninety-nine-percentist Left'.
6 Rapport sur les inégalités en France, Observatoire des inégalités, 2021.
7 Measured by household, wealth includes real estate, financial capital and professional assets (INSEE definition).
8 'In 2018, inequalities in standard of living increase' ('Revenu, niveau de vie et pauvreté en 2018', INSEE, 9 September 2020).

9 More frequent air travel and promotion of a metropolitan model that is largely responsible for the current ecocide.
10 In the 1930s, for example, Jean Renoir, the son of the painter Auguste Renoir (one could not be more in the hypercultural elite) made his film *La Bête humaine* with its idealization of that figure of the Popular Front, the railway worker.
11 See Chapter 4, note 2.
12 'People who succeed and people who are nothing': these were the words used on 29 June 2017 by Emmanuel Macron during the inauguration of Station F in Paris, the biggest start-up campus in Europe.

II The fog
1 The expression 'Potemkin village' refers to a trompe-l'oeil used for propaganda purposes. In 1787, according to historical legend, luxurious cardboard facades were erected in the Crimea at the request of the Russian minister Grigori Potemkin, in order to hide the poverty of the villages during the visit of Empress Catherine II.

4 Cinema
1 Shlomo Sand, *The Invention of the Jewish People*, translated by Yael Lotan (London: Verso, 2010).
2 Marcel Gauchet 'L'idée que le passé peut être remodelé à volonté est une idée totalitaire', *Le Figaro*, 20 October 2017.
3 Ibid.
4 Ibid.
5 Pier Paolo Pasolini, *Écrits corsaires* (Paris: Champs Flammarion, 2018); *Contre la télévision et autres textes sur la politique et la société* (Paris: Les Solitaires intempestifs, 2003); 'La télévision, une des manifestations les plus tapageuses de cette culture de masse que le capitalisme impose', https://comptoir.org/ (the website of *La Revue du Comptoir*).
6 Pier Paulo Pasolini, 'Défi aux dirigeants de la télévision', *Corriere della sera*, 9 December 1973.

7 'Le journal du confinement', Leïla Slimani, *Le Monde*, March 2020.
8 'Journal d'une confinée', Marie Darrieussecq, *Le Point*, March 2020.
9 'Brigitte Macron éprouvée par le confinement', *Gala*, 27 March 2020.
10 Sixty per cent of teleworkers are executives, while they only represent twenty per cent of employees. In 2021, INSEE specifies that on average, each week, 55 per cent of executives teleworked, while this was the case for only 22 per cent of intermediate professions and seventeen per cent of qualified employees. Telework was almost non-existent throughout the year among low-skilled employees or workers.
11 'Ces viviers où prolifèrent les experts médiatiques', *Le Monde diplomatique*, December 2019. (Terra Nova is a French think tank, as are the Institut Montaigne and the Fondation Jean-Jaurès. – Translator's note.)
12 Éric Neuhoff, *(Très) Cher cinéma français* (Paris: Albin Michel, 2019).
13 A French soap-opera set in Marseilles. (Translator's note.)
14 Jean-Claude Michéa, *Le Loup dans la bergerie* (Paris: Champs Flammarion, 2019).
15 'Un inépuisable mythe en temps d'extrême adversité', *Le Monde diplomatique*, February 1993.
16 Chantal Jaquet, *Les transclasses ou la non-reproduction* (Paris: PUF, 2014).
17 In the press, in a book, on the radio or on television.
18 The Italian film *Brutti, sporchi e cattivi* (*Ugly, Dirty and Bad*) directed by Ettore Scola and released in 1976, tells the daily life of a family in a shanty town in Rome. About twenty people – parents, children, their spouses or lovers, grandchildren and the grandmother – are crammed into a sordid hovel, living off petty theft and prostitution, under the tyrannical authority of the one-eyed, greedy and violent patriarch.
19 Alain Finkielkraut's expression.

20 Jack London, *What Life Means to Me*, published in 1906, available online at https://upload.wikimedia.org/wikipedia/commons/e/ec/Jack_London%27s_%22What_life_means_to_me.%22_%28IA_jacklondonswhatl00londrich%29.pdf.
21 J. D. Vance, *Hillbilly Elegy: A Memoir of a Family and Culture in Crisis* (New York: Harper Press, 2016). See also 'États-Unis: Vance, le "Hillbilly" de Trump dans l'Ohio', *Le Figaro*, 12 May 2022.
22 *Hillbilly Elegy*, directed by Ron Howard and released in 2020, received the Oscar for best supporting actress for Glenn Close.
23 J. D. Vance, 'Opioid of the Masses', *The Atlantic*, 4 July 2016, available online at https://www.theatlantic.com/politics/archive/2016/07/opioid-of-the-masses/489911/.
24 'Saint-Denis Connection', *Les Échos*, 9 April 2016.
25 In this, it is aided and abetted by Macronism.
26 *Insee Première*, n° 1804, July 2020.
27 'Les dispositifs zonés de soutien du développement économique et de l'emploi dans les territoires', Inspection générale des finances, IGAS, July 2020.

5 'There is no majority'

1 Pierre George, *Dictionnaire de la géographie* (Paris: PUF, 1984).
2 Vidal de La Blache (1845–1918) produced a *Tableau de la géographie de la France* (*Tableau of the Geography of France*) (Paris: La Table ronde, 1994); Élisée Reclus (1830–1905) wrote the *Histoire d'un ruisseau (History of a Stream)* (Paris: Babel, 2005); Edmond Bernus (1929–2004) wrote *Touaregs, un peuple du désert (The Touaregs, a desert people)* (Paris: Grandvaux, 2007).
3 The NUPES (New Ecological and Social People's Union) was a short-lived alliance of left-wing parties (2022–24). (Translator's note.)
4 The majority of executives vote NUPES (28%), the majority of workers vote for the National Rally (45%), with Macronism attracting a majority of retirees (35%). Source Ipsos.
5 'Législatives 2022: en raison de la forte abstention, des députés

parfois élus par moins de 10% des inscrits', *Le Monde*, 20 June 2022.
6 Stephen R. Soukup, *The Dictatorship of Woke Capital. How Political Correctness Captured Big Business* (New York: Encounter Books, 2012).
7 'Terra Nova: il y a dix ans la note qui fracturait la gauche et pavait la voie à Macron', *Marianne*, 9 May 2021. (For Terra Nova, see Chapter 4, note 11, above.)
8 Christophe Guilluy, *Twilight of the Elites: Prosperity, the Periphery, and the Future of France*, translated by Malcolm DeBevoise (New Haven, CT and London: Yale University Press, 2019), p. 45.
9 '1er tour: comprendre le vote des Français', 10 April 2022, Ipsos.
10 As shown, for example, by the significant percentages obtained by the National Rally in overseas France.
11 Bertolt Brecht, 'The solution', a poem written in 1953.
12 'Ces musulmans qui plébiscitent l'école catholique', *Le Figaro*, 18 February 2014.
13 'Une prime de fidélisation de 10 000 € versée aux agents publics exerçant en Seine-Saint-Denis', Portail de la fonction publique, October 2020.
14 Jean-Laurent Cassely and Jérôme Fourquet, *La France sous nos yeux* (Paris: Seuil, 2022).
15 'La country, c'est la liberté, c'est comme une Harley sur la route 66', *Le Monde*, 18 December 2021.

6 Apocalypse now

1 *Charles Baudelaire*, 'The Generous Player', in *Poems in Prose*, translated by Joseph T. Shipley, available online at https://www.gutenberg.org/files/47032/47032-h/47032-h.htm.
2 The Évin law, passed in 1991, increased the restrictions on tobacco and alcohol advertising. (Translator's note.)
3 *Dimanche en politique*, France 3.
4 This is a reference to the paedophilia trial that took place in

Outreau, northern France, from 1997 to 2000. (Translator's note.)
5 In 2021 Olivier Duhamel, a prominent political scientist, confessed to sexually abusing his stepson in the latter's early teens. (Translator's note.)
6 The European Treaty of Maastricht was narrowly ratified in 1992.
7 'L'alternance unique', an expression used by Jean-Claude Michéa.
8 The European Constitutional Treaty of 2005.
9 According to the annual report 'Fractures françaises', Ipsos.
10 Figures from the French Ministry of the Interior.
11 'Élections américaines 2020: un nombre de voix historique pour Biden, mais aussi pour Trump', *Le Monde*, 8 November 2020.
12 In 2022, 'Earth Overshoot Day', which marks the moment when humanity has consumed all the resources that ecosystems can produce in a single year, fell on July 28.
13 'Le modèle néolibéral, une nuisance pour l'environnement?', *Le Devoir*, 6 October 2016.
14 'Accord commercial Union européenne-Nouvelle Zélande: ouvrir la voie à une croissance économique durable', Commission européenne, 30 June 2022.

7 The radical nature of ordinary life
1 'Les offres d'emploi non pourvues restent, selon une étude, un phénomène "marginal"', *Le Monde*, 11 February 2022.
2 *Zadig*, 28 May 2021.
3 'Incidents au Stade de France: le déni des pouvoirs publics malgré une organisation défaillante', *Le Monde*, 30 May 2022.
4 Jérôme-Sainte Marie, *Bloc populaire* (Paris: Éditions du Cerf, 2021).
5 'Aux Pays-Bas, la colère des agriculteurs devient l'image d'une périphérie qui subit', *Le Figaro*, 13 July 2022.
6 In May 2017, the situation was serious. The stability of the system and therefore of heritage was at stake. Ignoring their 'values',

the bourgeoisies did not tremble: the conservative bourgeoisie gave its votes to the very progressive Macron; the progressive bourgeoisie, although very angry with this 'candidate of finance', did not hesitate either.
7 In 2022, on TF1, the election night of the first round of the presidential election was very short and followed by the umpteenth broadcast of the 1993 comedy *Les Visiteurs (The Visitors)*.
8 The pinnacle was reached with the renovation of La Samaritaine in Paris.
9 A hard-discount is a self-service store with a predominance of food which is characterized by below-average sales prices, a small sales area and a limited product assortment.

8 Not against but elsewhere

1 Jacques Julliard, 'La campagne électorale a pris la forme d'un insupportable huis clos', *Le Figaro*, 1 May 2022.
2 Ibid.
3 BETC is Babinet Erra Tong Cuong Euro RSCG, a famous French communications agency created in the 1990s and now the fourth largest agency in the sector worldwide.
4 Pierre-André Taguieff, *Résister au bougisme* (Paris: Fayard, 2001).
5 Charles Maurras (1868–1952) was a right-wing monarchist writer. (Translator's note.)
6 'Des Gilets jaunes aux grandes réformes, les consultants en première ligne du quinquennat', *Le Monde*, 17 March 2022.
7 The annual World Economic Forum or Davos Forum (in Switzerland) is the largest private gathering of elites on the planet.
8 Jérôme Sainte-Marie, *Bloc contre bloc* (Paris: Lexio, 2020).
9 This expression was used by Emmanuel Macron and Bruno Le Maire during the Covid pandemic in 2020.
10 In thirty years, nearly half of post offices, nearly forty per cent of maternity wards, thirty per cent of train stations, thirty per cent of tax offices, 25 per cent of schools, fifty per cent of Banque de

France branches and judicial courts have closed. See Aleksandra Barczak and Mohamed Hilal, *Quelle évolution de la présence des services publics?* (Rennes: Presses universitaires de Rennes, 2016).
11 The size of screens in houses, regularly mentioned, reinforces the image of the 'redneck' slumped in front of his television; what people omit to mention is that the biggest consumers of screens and media (Internet and platforms) are in reality the upper social classes. See Media in Life on the website Médiamétrie (2019), available online at https://www.mediametrie.fr/en/media-life.
12 The top two items of expenditure for the wealthiest are transportation and goods and services, while housing and food are those of the poorest. Source: INSEE.
13 Ipsos consumption figures, 14 June 2022.
14 The despair expressed when a social plan or a factory closure hits peripheral France is a sad illustration of this.
15 'Insécurité et délinquance en 2021', French Ministry of the Interior.
16 Jean-Claude Michéa, *L'Empire du moindre mal* (Paris: Champs Flammarion, 2021).

9 Return to the centre

1 According to Charles Péguy, 'Kantian ethics has clean hands but, in a manner of speaking, actually no hands', quoted in Monad Rrenban, *Wild, Unforgettable Philosophy In Early Works of Walter Benjamin* (Lanham, MD: Lexington Books, 2005), p. 210.
2 Honoré de Balzac, *La Peau de chagrin*, published in 1831; English translation by Ellen Marriage, available online at https://www.gutenberg.org/cache/epub/1307/pg1307-images.html. (In this novel, every time the hero makes a wish, the magic piece of shagreen leather that he possesses grants him the wish, but shrinks – and his life shortens. – Translator's note.)
3 The term idiocracy is used to describe a government that is governed by incompetent, even imbecilic, figures.

4 Nassim Nicholas Taleb, 'The Intellectual Yet Idiot', available online at https://medium.com/incerto/the-intellectual-yet-idiot-13211e2d0577#.3v9bolkbw.
5 The École national d'administration was dissolved in 2021. (This elite school had trained many members of France's political elite. – Translator's note.)
6 'Le jury de l'Ena décrit des candidats moutonniers, incapables de penser par eux-mêmes', *Marianne*, 2 March 2018.
7 Ibid.
8 For example, forgetting that, in the 1930s, Joseph Goebbels had not seduced just a mass of morons, but on the contrary the intellectuals and industrialists of one of the most educated European countries of the time, 'intelligent idiots' spend their time warning of the imminent danger of the return of a brutality they claim is intrinsic to ordinary people.
9 'Les Français doivent-ils avoir peur de la démondialisation?', *Le Figaro*, 6 June 2022.
10 'La nouvelle mort annoncée de la mondialisation', *Le Devoir*, 15 April 2022.
11 Fyodor Mikhailovich Dostoyevsky, *The Dream of a Ridiculous Man*, first published in 1877, translated by Constance Garnett, available online at https://www.online-literature.com/dostoevsky/3368/.
12 Oswald Spengler, *The Decline of the West*, edited by Arthur Helps and Helmut Werner, translated by Charles F. Atkinson (New York: Oxford University Press, 1991).
13 'Occident et mondialisation', Fondation Res Publica, 21 January 2013.
14 Samuel P. Huntington, *The Clash of Civilizations and the Remaking of World Order* (New York: Simon and Schuster, 1996).
15 Fondation Res Publica, 4 October 2018.
16 Hubert Védrine, *Une vision du monde* (Paris: Bouquins, 2022).
17 Brazil, Russia, India, China, South Africa represent 45 per cent of the world population and a quarter of the world economy. In

2050, China will become the leading economic power, ahead of the United States.
18 De-dollarization is the substitution of the US dollar as the currency used for oil and raw materials trading and trade agreements.
19 For Spengler, imbued with the superiority complex of the Westerners of his time, the history of Western Europe was a willed destiny, while India's destiny was merely a matter of happenstance.
20 Contrary to what is asserted, the 'weakness' of the Western world is not the ageing of its population: this process concerns all of humanity, particularly Asia, which is economically coming out on top, but it temporarily excludes Africa.
21 Michel Houellebecq, *Annihilation*, translated by Shaun Whiteshead (London: Picador, 2024).
22 This is part of the dialogue in the film *Taxi for Tobruk* (1961), directed by Denys de La Patellière (written by Michel Audiard).
23 'La violence par armes à feu, un fléau qui inquiète la Suède', *Le Monde*, 10 December 2021.
24 'La Suède freine sur la question du changement de sexe des mineurs', *RTS*, 27 June 2021.
25 German energy policy, in order to be faithful to its environmental dogmas, closed its nuclear power plants, favoured renewable energies and, ultimately, reopened extraction mines and coal-fired power plants (with, as a result, the worst carbon footprint in Europe).

Epilogue
1 'La baisse d'attractivité des métropoles est confirmée', *Insee Analyses* no. 81, 16 March 2023.
2 'Personne ne devrait être abandonné à l'enfer du béton!', *Usbek & Rica*, 24 June 2022.
3 Gérard-François Dumont, *Les Territoires français: diagnostic et gouvernance* (Paris: Armand Colin, 2018).